A Commentary on
EPHESIANS

UNLOCKING THE NEW TESTAMENT

A Commentary on
EPHESIANS

David Pawson

Anchor Recordings

First published in Great Britain in 2016 by
Anchor Recordings Ltd
72 The Street, Kennington, Ashford TN24 9HS

**For more of David Pawson's teaching,
including DVDs and CDs, go to
www.davidpawson.com**

**FOR FREE DOWNLOADS
www.davidpawson.org**

**For further information, email
info@davidpawsonministry.org**

ISBN 978-1-909886-98-8

Printed by Lightning Source

Contents

This book is based on a series of talks. Originating as it does from the spoken word, its style will be found by many readers to be somewhat different from my usual written style. It is hoped that this will not detract from the substance of the biblical teaching found here.

As always, I ask the reader to compare everything I say or write with what is written in the Bible and, if at any point a conflict is found, always to rely upon the clear teaching of scripture.

David Pawson

THE CHRISTIAN'S WEALTH

Read Ephesians 1

A. THE GREETING (1)

B. THE GRACE (3–8)
1. Showered with blessings (3)
2. Chosen for holiness (4)
3. Destined as sons (5–6)
4. Forgiven through blood (7–8)

C. THE GOAL (9–10)
1. Insight (9)
2. Integration (10)

D. PRAISE OF GOD (11–14)
1. We – His purpose
   Hoped, destined, appointed
2. You – His promise
   Heard, believed, sealed

E. POWER OF GOD (15–23)
1. Paul prays (15–19)
   a. Wisdom of His mind
   b. Wealth of His magnificence
   c. Working of His might
2. Paul preaches (20–22)
   a. Resurrection (Ascension and exaltation)
   b. Realm (space and time)
   c. Rule (world and church)

1:1–10

I expect you know how pearls are formed in oysters. A pearl begins to grow when a little piece of grit finds its way inside the shell of an oyster and begins to irritate and rub against the soft flesh inside. So the oyster, to protect itself, begins to secrete a hard substance around the grit and that grows, and it becomes a beautiful and precious thing – and it all started under those irritating circumstances. Among the letters of Paul, his letter to the Ephesians is the pearl of great price. It has been called by commentators "the queen of all the epistles". But you need to remember that this lovely pearl was formed in irritating circumstances. The writer of this letter is in a prison cell, chained permanently to a guard from whom he can never get away. He is shut off from his friends and loved ones. An active, open air man, he is now shut in, and he writes a letter like this. It is a pearl that was produced under the irritating circumstances of imprisonment, as if the most precious things that God can say to people come to them when their earthly circumstances are very hard. It seems that God is able to do this – when we go through rough and difficult times he speaks to us words that are more precious than anything he says when everything is going smoothly.

The theme of this letter to the Ephesians is *the purpose of God*. Like a twined flax, there are two strands. Strand number one is God's plan and so is number two – God's power. God not only has a plan, he has the power to put it into operation. The whole epistle is concerned with the purpose of God that is going to be fulfilled because he has a plan and the power to complete it. You find these two words, *purpose* and *power*, coming again and again. The letter itself divides up very clearly into two parts right down the middle – chapters one to three and chapters four to six.

Broadly speaking, we can say this: the first part of the letter is concerned with the salvation that God works in. The second half is concerned with the salvation that you work out. The first half is concerned with belief, the second half with behaviour; the first half with your experience of Christ and the second half with your example to others; the first half with worship and witness and the second half with your walk and your warfare. The first half, what we are saved *by*, the second half what we are saved *for*; the first half *adoration*, the second half *application*.

So in the first half we are concerned with our relationship to God, our salvation in Christ, the beauty and the wonder of God's purpose and power as they are being worked out in our life. We start with the first ten verses.

The introduction in the first two verses is a very straightforward typical introduction of Paul to a letter, and I will just pick out four words. The word *apostle* literally means "sent". Paul makes it quite clear that he is sent not by his own choice but by God's choice, by the will of God. This means that every word we read of Paul's we accept not as Paul's but as God's. He is not here to speak his own opinion. He is writing to tell people what God says. Happy are those who accept the apostle's word as God's word. That is why he starts this way.

He didn't want to be an apostle; he had no ambition to be a missionary. He didn't want to go and spread the gospel. It was furthest from his thoughts as a young man. His ambition was to kill the gospel dead, but God had other plans. I was called to be a preacher by the will of God. I didn't want to be one; I had no desire to get up into a pulpit. I wanted to be a farmer, but God had other plans. But when God sends you, you go, and you can do no other. I am not an apostle, but by the grace of God I am a teacher. Paul was an apostle. That is a great and honourable calling, but it was God who chose him. So we read this letter not as a letter from a man, but as a letter from God.

Secondly, notice the word *saints*. If ever I had a chance to talk with the Pope I think I would want to tell him that we have as many saints in our local church as he claims to have in the entire Roman Catholic Church, because I believe we are all saints. God calls you "saint". There are not a few special people who have been canonised by somebody. God says, "If you believe in Jesus you're one of my saints. I see you in him, I see you as you're going to be, I see you as he will make you. You're my saint." So Paul says, "I'm an apostle," and that privilege was the privilege of few. But he says, "You're a saint" – and that is the privilege of many.

He adds one qualification. He says, "I'm writing to the saints that are faithful." Do you know that the work and witness of every church depends on the faithful saints? What lovely people they are, those of whom you can say, "It doesn't matter what the weather, I know they will be there if they possibly can. If you ask them to do something, they will do it." Those who are faithful saints – thank God for them, they keep us all going, "To the saints that are faithful...."

Now two other words: *grace* and *peace*. "Grace" was the Greek or Gentile form of greeting and it meant, "May the favour of the gods be upon you." It was a kind of Gentile cheer-up. "Peace" was the Jewish greeting, which meant harmony, peacefulness, "May you be in harmony." It was as much as to say: I take the Gentile and the Jewish greeting and in Christ you can put them together; the favour of God's will be upon you, God the Father, God the Son, and God the Holy Spirit, and the peace of God which passes all understanding will be yours; grace and peace be to you.

You notice that he puts God and Jesus on an equal plane.

Both of them will do it for you. Those who don't yet see Jesus Christ as God need to look at this phrase, "Grace to you and peace from God and from Jesus" – no distinction, no grading. They are equal in Paul's sight. So he says grace and peace from them both. That is the greeting.

We move into vv. 3–10. In the Greek, vv. 3–14 is only one sentence and I defy you to analyse it grammatically. Nobody has yet been able to discover the main clause in it. It tumbles out like a torrent of words, as if Paul is so full that he can't string his words together properly. The Holy Spirit is no respecter of grammar any more than persons. He is saying that the grammar of the Greek language can't contain the blessings that God has poured into my life. It just flows – phrase after phrase builds up and there is repetition as certain key words keep coming. The key word that occurs most frequently (fourteen times in just one sentence) is "in". It is the most important word there: "in" him; in Christ; in the Beloved – in, in, in.

As soon as you step into Christ, things begin to happen – as soon as you're in him. Not just Christ in you, but *you in Christ* since he is the greater and the lesser is in the greater. You are in him. You are actually living in Christ. In baptism, says Paul, you have put on Christ – as you put on your clothes. Living in him, a torrent of things begin to happen. This sentence is written by a man who feels like a millionaire. Look at some of the extravagant language. He talks of God lavishing things on us, of the riches of his grace, which he freely bestowed. God's the big spender – that is what Paul is saying here.

God, the biggest spender of all who lavished upon us, who poured out upon us blessings, showered us with them. Paul is really feeling wealthy here, and no wonder. I want you to notice that this whole passage teaches you to look at things from God's point of view, not from man's. We are so prone to think of our salvation from our point of view, what *we* got out of it. But let us think of what God is going to get out of it. Look at it from his point of view. Why did he spend so much on us? What was he hoping to achieve? Why was he so reckless in blessing us? Well, we will see from God's point of view why we began to be saved, what it is all about. Let us realise that God has a purpose and a plan that he is unfolding before our very eyes.

The God we're talking about is the only God there is, the God and the Father of our Lord Jesus – there is no other. Every other god who is worshipped is a figment of the imagination. There is no other God, therefore there is no other religion but the Christian religion. The rest are all a delusion. Blessed be the God and Father of our Lord Jesus Christ, that is the God there is, and there is no other. Now let us look at this torrent of words.

First of all, let's look at the *grace* that has come to us. That is a word you rarely hear used outside the church, except in a very different sense, meaning beauty or charm or grace of movement. It is even rarely used in that sense now. But Christians love the word "grace". If you want to get the flavour of it, I think I would have to translate it "generosity". It means to give, to give, and to give again freely – not asking for things in return, just wanting to give. The grace of God is his generosity. We live in a day when one phrase that attracts people is "free gift". With God, the free gift of God is eternal life. That is grace – you didn't deserve it, you didn't buy it, you didn't have to pay for it. It is free. This is the grace that Paul is now going to talk about: blessed us, bestowed on us, lavished.

Here are ways God has showered us with blessings. First: *every* blessing. I hope you will underline your Bible as we go through Ephesians. Don't mind doing that, get out a pen now and underline the word "every". It is rather as though when I was a child a wealthy uncle from Australia had come and visited our home and said, "Come on, I'll take you out shopping," and took me into a toy shop and said, "You can have everything." Everything! Can you imagine how a child's eyes would light up?

The tragedy is that when we grow up we can become so blasé about gifts. Fancy a child going into a toyshop and being told, "You don't need to choose, you can have everything, the lot," and the wealthy uncle signing a cheque for everything in the shop: "There you are!" You would hardly know where to begin.

Paul is saying that he hasn't only blessed you with *some* blessings, he has given you everything he has in his store in heaven—the lot! There isn't a thing that God doesn't own that you won't one day inherit in Christ. Joint heirs with him, everything's coming to you. Now that is quite something — we can hardly understand it.

Let us ask a few questions about these blessings we have received. What are they? They are *spiritual* blessings. Quite frankly, to the unbeliever that wouldn't cause any excitement whatever. The unbeliever wants material blessings or social blessings, but these are not promised here. Materially and socially you may be poor, that is not the kind of blessing that God has given us. Remember the man writing this was in prison; he had no material blessings, no social blessings. He even had to write a letter to ask someone to bring an overcoat to keep him warm, yet he says, "Blessed be the God and Father of our Lord Jesus ... every spiritual blessing."

Spiritual blessings are the things you come to value when you come to be in Christ. Before that, you weren't interested in spiritual things, they didn't excite you. But now, spiritual blessings—love, joy, peace, these are the things that he has given you. Every blessing he has is now down on your account over your name and you can draw on those things.

Blessed be God who has blessed us with every spiritual blessing. Where are these blessings? They are not in earthly places, they are in heavenly places. Once again the world will say, "Well, I'm not interested. I want my blessings here and now. I'm like Esau, I'd rather have a plate of soup now than something away up there." The world laughs and says, "Pie in the sky when you die." Well, I don't mind pie in the sky. I have often said, "That's better than pain in the pit when you flit." Let the world laugh. The blessings are in the heavenly places. Quite frankly, they are much safer there. The more blessings you have in earthly places the more you worry about them. The more stocks and shares you have, the more you will be worried about financial markets. This is where moth and rust corrupt and where thieves break in and steal. This is where your treasures are not safe. This is where inflation can run off with them just like that. Thank God that our blessings are not in earthly places, they are in a much safer place; they are in the heavenly places.

Now how can I have these blessings if they are in heavenly places and I am in an earthly place? The answer is: the more I learn to live in the heavenly place the more blessings I can have now. Can you see that? The more earthly you are and the more worldly you get and the more attached you are to things down here, the less of your heavenly blessings can you enjoy now. But the more you learn to live in the heavenly places now and seek the things that are above and let your mind dwell on where Christ is seated at the right hand of the Father, the more blessings you can have right now, because you are living in the heavenly places even while you move around earth. You can sit on a bus and be in the heavenly places and enjoy your blessings. You can do the washing up and be in the heavenlies and enjoy the heavenly blessings. That is where they are.

When will we get all these? The answer is that he has

blessed us with every spiritual blessing so you have got the lot now. That doesn't mean that you already have actual possession of it all. In v. 14 we read, "... the guarantee of our inheritance, until we acquire possession of it," so there is more to come. How did it come to be ours? The answer is: in Christ. You will find this phrase, and this word "in", as we go through this study – in him. The tragedy is that the world is trying to get these blessings outside of Christ. No wonder they can't find them. The world is trying to find peace outside Christ, love outside Christ, joy outside Christ, and they are all to be found in him. That is why we are eternally frustrated. We sing about love, but we somehow can't find it, and we work for peace and somehow it doesn't come and war breaks out again. We try to be joyful and somehow we are left with a hangover. It is because we are trying to find it all outside Christ. How do you get these blessings? Blessed be the God and Father of our Lord Jesus who has blessed us with every spiritual blessing in Christ. Once you have got him, you have got the rest.

I remember an old fable about a monkey trying to lift something out of a narrow-neck jar. He put his paw in and got hold of it but couldn't pull it out. The very simple answer was take the jar and then you have got everything. Take Christ – and all the blessings that are in him are yours. Why? Why did God do all this, showered blessings upon us, *every* blessing? Let us move to the next verse: chosen for *holiness*. If someone asked you, "When did you begin to be a Christian?" your answer will depend on whether you look at their question from a human point of view or from God's point of view. From man's point of view you would say, "Well, in my case, it was in the month of September and it was in the year 1947 and I chose Christ as my Saviour and I began the Christian life." That is from a human point of view. But if you ask me when I began to be a Christian from God's point of view do you know what my answer will be? Before the planet earth was made God chose me in him—there it is again. Now this idea of predestination is an offence to the unbelieving mind of man. He will argue about it from now to doomsday. He finds it an offence to his freedom. He wants to be free, and so he doesn't want God to have freewill; *he* wants to make the choices, not God himself. But for those who have come to be in Christ, predestination becomes a most precious and lovely truth.

Jesus taught his disciples: you thought you chose me; you didn't choose me, I chose you. If you could have asked Simon Peter when he began the Christian life, I think I know what Peter would have said: "One day Jesus came to me and he said, 'Peter, I have chosen you."

If you are a Christian, look back now and see how God showed before you became a Christian that he wanted you, spoke to you, tenderly drew with the cords of love, arranged for you to meet certain people, arranged that you should be at a certain place at a certain time. Look how he did that! He wooed you and he won you. When did he first decide to have you? The answer is: before he made the earth. That is when he decided. To me, it is the security of my soul to know that he wanted me before it all began. Blessed be God who chose us in him.

I remember somebody saying to me once, "I knew you when you were just a gleam in your father's eye." I didn't understand the phrase at the time but I understand it now. I know now that I am the result of my earthly father's love and decision to have a family. But I also know that I am the result of a decision of my heavenly Father to have a family, and he chose us in him before the foundation of the earth. In other words, God planned people before things. I know this earth was here before I was here, but not in God's mind. In God's mind he didn't create the planets first and then say,

"Now, let's think about it. I think I'll put some human beings on that planet." No, he made the world with people in mind.

Let us move on from there. To the Christian the great question is not "How can you fit in predestination with free will?" You can argue about that until the cows come home, it won't do you much spiritual good. The great question is: why? Why did he choose me, why did he want me? What aim did he have in mind? The answer comes: he wanted perfect people and he has chosen me to be one of his perfect people. That almost takes my breath away. What about you? How do you feel?

You see, human nature is not perfect. "No-one is perfect," says the world, and that is true. By nature no-one is perfect, but God wanted some perfect people and he chose us in him to be holy and blameless before him, that he might look down and say, "There, isn't that a perfect child?" – that we might reflect his own holiness, blameless; he chose me to be blameless. That is an amazing word – somebody you couldn't find fault with. That is not me by nature.

Which moves us on to the next thing, we are destined *as sons*. Somebody asked me this, "Why did God create man?" My answer was, "Because he wanted a bigger family." God the Father already had one Son and he loved him so much that he called him "My Beloved" – the only begotten Son. But, being love, he wanted a bigger family to share things with. So he was going to have more sons. There is one big difference between Christ's sonship and ours, and it is that he was begotten but we are adopted.

These are the two ways into a family: to be born into the family, begotten into it, or to be adopted. We are adopted into God's family and there are some lovely things about adoption. One of them is that with adoption every child is chosen and wanted. When you have been adopted by God the Father you can be quite sure you were wanted in his family.

So he said, "I will adopt you and you and you." Destined as sons in his love – the whole thing sprang from love; we are drenched in love.

Again, you notice this happens *in* the Beloved. Every time the little word "in" is put in, because outside of Christ none of this is true. Not one whit of this will happen to those *outside* of Christ, but to those who are in the Beloved. This means that not all people are sons of God. Not everyone has the right to call God "Father". The New Testament is crystal clear: only in Christ do you receive the right to become sons of God and to call him your Father. Nobody who is outside of Christ can use the Lord's Prayer. It is impossible, "Our Father...." We are destined to be his sons in the Beloved.

The next blessing—and here is the climax—the most generous act of God. One thing could have spoiled all the rest; one thing could have hindered it, one thing could have kept me from being a son of God. That thing would be sin or "trespasses". What does to trespass mean? It means to climb over a fence into someone else's property. It means to go where you are forbidden to go. It means to do what you have been told not to do, and every one of us has trespassed.

The most generous thing God ever did was to forgive our trespasses. Can you imagine living with a holy God with unforgiven sin? Can you imagine going around with a guilty conscience, knowing that God knows everything you have done, knowing that it is there all the time? Can you imagine the hell of that? But God says, "I've forgiven." Now it wasn't easy for God to forgive. It was a costly thing, it was through blood. "In whom we have redemption through his blood, the forgiveness of our trespasses." Never forget that it cost the blood of Jesus to get your trespasses forgiven. That is why we go on drinking wine so regularly in church that we might never forget the blood of Jesus—*set free*.

Now I want to underline at this point what your life

would be like outside of Christ. Firstly, you would have no spiritual blessings in the heavenly places. Let me spell that out in simple terms. It means that the day you die you lose everything. All your blessings are in earthly places if you are outside of Christ. When you die you leave every blessing behind, there isn't one you can take with you. You may have many material blessings on earth, but if you have no spiritual blessings in the heavenlies you are desperately poor.

Alas, one wants to shout that in places where people have so many material blessings in earthly places. You want to say, "You're going to say goodbye to all of it!" Two people were talking about a rich man after he had died. One said, "How much did he leave?" and the other said, "Everything." They go to the next world in poverty with not a single blessing to look forward to – not one. A man or a woman may be comfortable and rich here and have all the blessings of health and friends that they could ask for, but the tragedy is that they are going to lose the lot outside of Christ. They have no blessing to look forward to.

Secondly, of course, it means that they will never be perfect. They will have to live with themselves for all eternity. The astronomer Fred Hoyle reckoned that he didn't want to live longer than three hundred years. He couldn't stand the thought of living forever. No wonder, because outside of Christ you've got to live with yourself forever in an imperfect state, with all your faults, with all your weaknesses. The older you grow the more you get sick of yourself, don't you?

When you set off in life you wanted to be a great person, you had an ideal. You were going to make of life something that nobody else had made of life. Then by middle age you realised your own limitations. A book was published which propounded the theory that everybody rises to the level of incompetence, meaning that you will go up the ladder until you find you have gone too far and that you are not up to it, and then comes the moment of discovery and disillusionment that you are not going to get any further with life and you have got to live with your limitations. Outside of Christ you are limited to the frustration of the ideal you can never reach, and after a bit you just become cynical. Well, you accept it, you are not going make it; you will just settle down.

Thirdly, outside of Christ, you will never be a child of God. You will never know his family, you will never live in his home, and you will never call him Father outside of Christ. Outside of Christ you will have to live with your guilt and shame forever. There is no forgiveness, and your memory will bring back regret and remorse forever. Now that is the alternative. In Christ, every spiritual blessing, where it will be waiting for you when you die; in Christ, the hope of becoming the ideal person you long to be in your best moments; in Christ, the knowledge that you will live forever in a family of God's children in love. In Christ, the knowledge that your sins will be taken right away and gone forever and that you can face God with an open face.

When you think of what God has done for us you say, "Blessed be God," and the circuit of blessing is complete. Blessing has flowed both ways; God has showered us with blessings, so we now bless God. Blessed be God who has blessed us. Do you see the circuit? It is complete, and now life and love flow. That is how the circle of blessing is meant to flow. You see there are unbelievers who enjoy God's blessings without realising. He sends his sun on the good and the evil and his rain on the just and the unjust. But the cycle of blessing never gets completed. If they pray, it is always asking for something, and God is longing for praise and blessing himself. "Bless the Lord, O my soul, and forget not all his benefits." We are here to bless God. He blessed us. So Paul virtually tells us to complete the blessing.

Finally, let's look at vv. 9–10. What's it all about? Where is it all going? What has God got in mind for his ultimate plan? What is God after in all this? Why is he spending his grace so lavishly on us? What we have here is an insight into God's plan, and that is the one thing that man could never discover.

We can discover so much else through the telescope, through the microscope; we can discover the plan of the planets, we can see how they revolve around each other. But *why* do they revolve around each other? We can't discover that through the telescope. We can see *how* the atom works through the electron microscope, but *why* does the atom work? We might discover some things about human behaviour through psychology and sociology, but why are human beings here? We can't discover that. Man can discover so much, but he can't discover God's plan. But God in his infinite wisdom has shown us the plan, and Christians know what God's plan for the universe is. He has taught us so tenderly and so lovingly. He let us into the secret and he has said to every believer, "I'll tell you what my plan is and where you fit into it."

Verse ten tells us what the plan is. God's plan is a Christian universe. Let that stretch your imagination. Or to put it in the language here, "To unite all things in Christ, things in heaven and things on earth..." – that everything may one day be Christian. That is his plan, so that there is nothing outside of Christ in God's universe. What a plan! Beside that, man's plans, politicians' plans, look puny, laughable.

God's plan for the ages in the fullness of time is a Christian universe. Everything is going to be Christian, all things in Christ. It is interesting that man by himself cannot see any pattern in history. Many have tried; great historians have tried to discern the shape of events. But one of our great historians, H.A.L. Fisher, finally came to this conclusion at the end of one of his history volumes. He said: "In history there is no plot, no rhythm, no pattern—only one emergency following another." He studied human events and he said, "Where's it all going?" He was saying, "Nowhere, can't see it." Oscar Wilde, rather more cynically, called history a "criminal calendar". But Christians say that there is a plot, there is a rhythm, there is a pattern, and it is this: all the universe is going to be Christian.

As a Christian poet put it, "That one far off divine event to which the whole creation moves...." Can you see that? I can. In all the chaos of human events I can see this purpose. You read or watch media summaries of the important events and you think: how is it that these commentators, these communicators can't see the plot – that they see things that are unimportant in God's sight as big events, and they brush over things that to God's sight are part of the plan?

There are two things I see as I look at events. First: God's frustration of everything man tries to do outside Christ. Can you not see that plot? Every time man tries to achieve something outside of Christ it comes to nothing. That is part of the plan. God will not let man achieve peace outside of Christ, so every attempt at peace comes to nothing. Secondly, on the other hand, we see the fulfilment of everything that is done in Christ. Can you see those two things together? At the end of each year, looking back at war after war, suffering after suffering, you see written over it all: "Man fails."

Yet more people are hearing the gospel today than have ever heard it before. The Bible is available in more languages than it has ever been available in before. These are the significant events. God is calling out a people of every kindred and tribe and tongue. So I can see God's plan coming and I know that history is moving towards the complete collapse of human civilisation and the establishment of the kingdom of God on earth in Christ.

Now I see the plan. Thank God for telling me what it is all about. I am not lost any more; I am not bewildered by the year's events. I'm not afraid to go into another year even if the worst happens, because I can see the plan and he showed it to me – God's great plan.

1:11–23
From v. 15 to v. 23 is just one sentence. Paul again is just tumbling out the words to describe the power and the glory of God. We will study that in a moment.

I believe in God's free will. It seems to me that those who discuss this forget that God has a will and that he is free. In fact, I am going to be so bold as to say that only God is really free, because he is the only one whose will controls everything and who is without limitations on what he decides to do. So in all the modern cry for freedom, let us begin by realising that God is the only really free person, and if you want to find freedom you will find it by finding God.

Now, when we say somebody has a strong will we mean two things. On the one hand, we mean that they are able to decide upon a purpose, they know what they want to do, and on the other hand, we mean that they also have the power to do it. We talk about somebody having "willpower". It's not just to know what you want to do, it is to be able to do it, and God has a very strong will. That is why the theme of the letter to the Ephesians is the purpose and the power of God, his will.

Look back at chapter one. Verse one says, "Paul, an apostle of Jesus Christ by the will of God...." He didn't choose to be an apostle; God decided that and appointed him to be an apostle. Look at a little further down, v. 5, "He destined us in love to be his sons through Jesus Christ, according to the purpose of his will." You didn't decide to be a son of God, he decided that; he adopted you and he chose you. Look a little further down to v. 9, "For he has made known to us in all wisdom and insight the mystery of his will." There it is again, the secret of his will. You might never have known what he decided to do unless he had shared the secret with you.

Note v. 11, "In him, according to the purpose of him who accomplishes all things according to the counsel of his will." We have had a number of phrases here: the mystery of his will; the purpose of his will; the counsel of his will. What does that mean? It means that when God decides to do something he consults himself. He doesn't go around asking people. The only counsel he takes is the counsel of his will, so he has a chat with himself and decides to do something. That is what the phrase "the counsel of his will" means. It is according to the counsel of his will that we have been caught up in his plan and purpose and power.

I divide this passage into two parts. How do I come into the purpose of God? How do I become part of the plan? The answer is through *preaching*. And how do I find the power to fulfil his purpose? The answer is through *praying*. That is why there will never be a day when preaching and praying are out of date; these are the two ways that God has chosen. He brings people into his purpose through preaching. He brings people into his power through praying. Nothing could be simpler, and these are the two grand agents he uses.

By "preaching" I don't mean getting up in a pulpit. It includes that, but is much bigger than that. If I were standing with you and there were just the two of us and I was talking to you about Jesus, I would be preaching. According to the New Testament, Philip and an Ethiopian eunuch met each other and Philip preached to him. Wherever one person tells another about the purpose of God, that is preaching. So you can preach wherever you are; whether you are in a pulpit or on a bus or in a shop or in an office or in the street, you can preach. That will be the way God will bring people into his purpose.

What is his purpose? What is the grand plan? We saw that in v. 10. His plan is a Christian universe. What a big plan! We plan little things but God has a big plan. Some people have tried to plan a Christian community. They have planned a monastery or a commune and said, "We'll take a house and we'll live together as a Christian community." That's a little plan. It's not necessarily a bad one, but it is a small one. Some people have planned something rather bigger, and have hoped and worked for a Christian nation. Some of the early founders of our national life hoped that England would be a Christian nation. Well, that is quite a big ambition, but not big enough for God. Some people even dream of a Christian world in which one day everybody in the world will be Christian. That is quite a big dream, but it is not big enough for God. God's plan is that all things in space and on the planet Earth should be united in Christ, a Christian universe, in which even the stars are Christian as well as the people. So that is God's big plan. We are part of it.

Now I want to ask: how do we know that we have become part of God's plan? How do we know that we will be there in that Christian universe?—because if God wills it, it is going to be. If God has decided that his purpose is a united Christian universe, no-one can stop it happening. He has the power to fulfil his purpose. How do we know? How can we be sure? Look at vv. 11–14. Paul speaks of two groups of people: "we" and "you". Who is he referring to? The "we" could refer to the first Christians, we who first hoped in Christ. Or he may be meaning the apostles. Or, more likely, I think he is referring to the Jews: "we".

He is conscious all through this letter, and particularly in chapter two, of Jew and Gentile. The first Christians were all Jews. The first people to pin their hope in Christ were

Jewish, and most of the New Testament came from Jewish pens. All the twelve apostles were Jewish. "We who first pinned our hope on Christ" – I think he is saying, "We Jewish Christians." When he says "you" he doesn't just mean the second generation of Christians, he means, "You Gentiles, you in Ephesus, you have been caught up as well." To a Jew the most amazing thing is that there could be a purpose of God for the Gentiles. I am afraid they had got to the point where they thought there was only one nation on earth that was going to fit into God's plan, the chosen people. But God had a bigger plan than a plan for the Jews – to bring the Gentiles in as well.

Now let us look at what Paul says about "We who first hoped in Christ...." Three verbs – and I am picking up verbs all the way in this study: hoped; destined; appointed. Take the first word, Paul describes the beginning of their faith as we who *hoped in Christ*. That is not a bad definition of how to become a Christian. A Christian is someone who has pinned his hopes on Jesus – all the hopes you have for your own life, for the world you live in.

Everybody has hopes. We can't live without some hope that things will get better, that our lives will get better, that our world will get better. We are always hoping that each year will be a better year than the last. Others might pin their hopes on science, politics, education and other people, but we are those who say, "We pinned our hopes on Jesus. We believe that he is going to get us out of this mess."

Do you remember the road to Emmaus? Two very sad people were walking down the country lane, Jesus joined them and they didn't recognise him. He said, "Why are you so sad?" They said, "Well, we just lost a great friend. His name was Jesus, and we hoped that he would redeem Israel. We had pinned our hopes on this man and we had thought he will get us out of our trouble – and he is dead.

Jesus said, "Oh fools, slow of heart to believe! Can't you see that you were right to pin your hopes on this person? Can't you see that he is fulfilling them, that he is making it all come true?" And before another half hour had passed they saw it and they realised that to pin your hopes on Jesus is the right thing to do.

Now, having said, "We pinned our hopes on Jesus," Paul says something happened before we did that and something happened after we did that. Before we pinned our hopes on Jesus we had been destined to do so. You know, the day comes when you pin your hopes on Jesus. I remember the day in September 1947, when as a young man I put the hope of my future on Jesus. But now I know that long before that memorable Friday night I had been destined. It all started way back in the will of God.

What followed? Paul says when we pinned our hopes in Christ we were destined before that, and after it we were appointed. This is God's order. He destines, then we respond to our destiny and pin our hopes in Jesus, then he appoints us. To do what?—to live for the praise of his glory. That is what you are appointed to do. After you have pinned your hopes in Jesus you are appointed to live to the praise of his glory. Now there are three levels of human life. You can live for yourself and live for the indulgence and the pleasure that you want, or you can live for others and serve others in their need, and that is one step higher. Praise God there are people who are not Christians who live for the needs of others, and you will meet them as you move around. But there is a higher calling, something even better than that. It is amazing how many people think that if you have reached step number two you must be a Christian. But step number three is the Christian life: to live for the praise of his glory. You can live for yourself, you can live for others – but you are destined and pin your hopes in Christ and step number three is to live for the praise of his glory, so that people think about God when they meet you, they don't just think about you. If you live for the needs of others then they will think about you as a good person, but they will not think about God. But if you live for the praise of his glory, when they meet you they will find themselves disturbed, and thinking, "There must be a God, or this person wouldn't be like this – to the praise of his glory."

Now if you are going to live to the glory of God, that includes your mouth. It includes your lips, and that is how God is going to bring others into his purpose. You who have pinned your hope on Christ, God is going to use your lips to bring somebody else into his plan. Think of that—that you could be part of this ingathering of people from every kindred, tribe and tongue.

Now look at vv. 13–14. Paul says, "We pinned our hopes on Christ first, but then we live to the praise of his glory, and you heard from us and you believed, and you came into it too." That is how it is spreading, and it is spreading faster today than it has ever spread for two thousand years. Did you realise how fast it is going? There are more new Christians in the world every minute. It is marvellous. It is really building up so rapidly and it is all being done as people live to the praise of his glory and tell others they have pinned their hopes in Jesus. Others hear the good news and they believe and they are brought into God's purpose.

There are three stages in which you come into the *purpose* of God – three steps among others. You could list about six actually, but Paul doesn't always give them all. For example, he doesn't mention baptism and repentance here. But he does single out three very important stages. Firstly: you *heard*. I have never yet met a Christian who did not first hear. If they couldn't hear then somebody wrote it down for them, but it was through words that they came into the purpose of

God, and there is no other way in. You first hear the gospel, the good news that God wants you as his child and that he is prepared to rescue you from yourself. You heard it first. But that of itself does not do anything. Many people hear the gospel and they don't get caught into the purpose of God. They go to church, they hear a preacher, they have a Bible in their home, they may have read it when they were a child, but they don't get caught up in the purpose of God. Why not? Because you hear and then, secondly, you *believed*. This is not a head thing, though the head needs to understand, it is a heart thing because it is not belief in a system, it is not belief in an idea. It says you believed in him. It is a personal relationship, and you don't enter into an act of faith in a person without the heart being involved, without acting upon that, without committing yourself to that person.

I remember when a surgeon told me, "I want to do a major operation on you. I have to, to help you out of this trouble." I virtually had to say, "Yes, I'll sign away my life; I'll sign a paper; I'll give you complete freedom to do this, and set you free from any responsibility if anything goes wrong." I had to make an act of faith in a person and say, "Here you are, here am I, I'm trusting you and here I am today." Now that is what an act of faith is. You heard about Jesus, you heard the good news that God sent his Son to save you. To believe that is to say, "Here I am, Jesus, I sign everything away into your hands. Now you help me, you save me."

Step number three is a very important step regarding the future. You heard the word, you believed in him, you were *sealed with the Holy Spirit*. Now I want to be very careful at this point, and I can only say what I understand this to mean. Notice that already you are involved with the Trinity; you heard the good news, you believed in Jesus, now comes the third person of the Trinity to do something for you: to seal you with the Holy Spirit.

The two words he uses, "seal" and "guarantee", are very important words. Let me tell you what they mean. When someone bought something in the open market in ancient Greece, it might have been some time before they could cart it home if it was a big object. So the buyer would take out of his pocket some sealing wax, melt it and put it on the thing he had bought, take his signet ring and bang it down, and then he had sealed that object. It couldn't be sold, nobody else could have it. He would one day come and collect it.

Now when God seals with the Holy Spirit, he is stamping a life and saying, "That life is mine, and one day I'm going to come and collect it." It is a simple picture and a lovely one. God wants to seal you off and to say, "I want everybody to know you're mine. I want nobody to be in any doubt I have bought you. Even if I leave you where you are in the market place for the moment, I'm going to come and collect you. I've sealed you."

The other word used is "guarantee". What does that mean? In the ancient world, if I ordered twenty sacks of corn, the transaction would be guaranteed by a man giving me one sack to go on with as a proof, a first instalment, a kind of deposit or first payment. He would give me the one sack to take home, and because I had the one sack I would regard that as the guarantee that there were nineteen others on the way. That is the word "guarantee" used here – a pledge, a foretaste, an earnest. What God is saying here to us is this: When I stamp you with my Holy Spirit that is the first instalment of heaven; the first down payment; that is the foretaste. That is your guarantee that the rest is available because you have already got a bit of it.

Now what is he referring to in all this? I can only say that I believe there are many Christians today who have heard the word, who have believed the gospel, but have not been sealed with the Holy Spirit. It is clearly something absolutely definite, without any doubt, without any uncertainty. It is a definite act of the Holy Spirit that leaves the person themselves in no doubt whatever that they have got the first bit of heaven, that they are God's property, that he has made it absolutely clear to them by confirming them that they belong to him. You don't need faith to believe in a seal. You need faith before that, but when the seal is given, then quite frankly there is no doubt anymore.

I can find in the book of Acts at least five occasions which tell me what sort of thing it was – one of them at the beginning of the history of the Ephesian church.

On the day of Pentecost there were 120 people sealed, stamped. Peter was saying there could be no doubt about it, these are God's people – that which you see and hear. God has stamped them his, and now you know they are my people and you will have no doubt, for this is God's stamp upon them.

I turn over the pages and I come to Acts 8 and I find there some believers in Samaria who heard the gospel, who believed it with great joy, who saw the miracles of God. But Peter and John came down to Samaria to ask God to seal them, to stamp them with his Holy Spirit, and he did. There was no doubt that they belonged afterwards. I turn the pages to chapter nine and I find that Saul himself, later to become Paul, met Jesus on the Damascus Road. Oh, he believed in him then all right. Jesus said, "I am Jesus," and Paul was converted on that Damascus Road – he believed. But three days later, in a little room in a street that you can still walk down in Damascus, it says that God sealed him with his Holy Spirit and stamped him his. There was no doubt in Paul's mind.

I turn the next page and I find a Roman regimental sergeant major listening with his household to the gospel, hearing and believing, and then suddenly God confirms him too, and his family, and stamps him with the Holy Spirit. There is no doubt in Peter's mind: these are God's people, they must be – God has stamped them. He has sealed them in the same way he has sealed us, they must be his. We have got to baptise them even though they are Gentiles.

Turn the pages again and you come to Acts 19 where we are shown the start of the church at Ephesus to which this letter is addressed. Paul is there preaching to a group who have been studying the Old Testament thoroughly, who have got as far as repenting, and even to a baptism of John, but as of yet they do not know fully about Jesus. So Paul takes them and he preaches to them and they believe and they are baptised in the name of Jesus.

Does it stop there? Oh no. He says, "You were sealed." God sealed them with his Holy Spirit, stamped them with his own signet ring, gave them a first deposit, a foretaste of heaven, a little part of the new universe he is going to create. Before you have been sealed with the Spirit you simply have to believe you will be in that new world; afterwards you are sure you will be. You just know.

There are two implications here that are worth mentioning. The first is that God wants us to be sure, both of himself and our future. He doesn't want his children to be in any doubt about their destination. The second is that such assurance comes from the direct witness of the Spirit, not by indirect deductions from scripture, as many evangelicals seem to think. The apostle John agrees with Paul on this ("We know that we live in him and he in us, because he has given us of his Spirit", 1 John 4:13). And we sing about it:

> If one should ask of me, "How can I tell?"
> Glory to Jesus, I know very well –
> God's Holy Spirit with mine doth agree,
> Constantly witnessing: Jesus loves me.

Of course, all this is in the past tense ("you were") because Paul is referring to the beginning of their Christian life. He is not here discussing the need to go on in the Spirit to retain this assurance. Elsewhere he urges believers to live in the Spirit rather than in the old flesh and in the same context warns them: "If anyone is not continuing to have the Spirit of Christ he does not belong to Christ" (Romans 8:9, translating the present tense of "have" properly). He repeats the warning in 11:22 ("provided that you continue...").

The Holy Spirit was "promised", another word confirming God's "guarantee". So as long as we walk and live by the Spirit , we "know" we are heading for heaven. We have the divine deposit in our hearts, quite sure the rest will follow. Sons are also heirs, to the praise of God's glory.

We move on to the matter of God's *power*. The purpose of God comes to you through preaching – you hear, believe, and are sealed. But how do you tap the power of God to achieve the purpose? Paul says, "I pray for you". He doesn't just preach, he prays. I don't just talk to you about God; I talk to God about you. This is the double ministry that we all have. Don't just talk to people about God, talk to God about people. The two ministries will share with them purpose and the power of God. Now this prayer of Paul's is a very good Christian prayer. It has a thank you in it and a please, and the thank you comes before the please. That is the right order. Don't rush into God with a shopping list, "Please can I have this, this, this, and this." Come in first and say, "Thank you Lord for this, this, this," and then say please. Paul tells them what he prays for them. There are three dimensions to a full Christian life: faith, hope, and love and he prays that they may have all three. He says thank you to God when he hears of their faith in the Lord Jesus. He says thank you to God when he hears of their love for all the saints. But the one area in which he feels they are lacking is the area of hope.

I think this is still the most neglected of the three virtues of the Christian life. You will hear sermons about faith and love but you don't hear so many about hope. What is hope? Faith reaches into the past and grasps the death and resurrection of Christ. Love reaches into the present and grasps the fellowship of the people of God. But hope is an anchor within the veil, it reaches into the future. It is the thing that anchors you to what is going to happen. If you only live for what Christ can do for you now, you are missing a whole dimension of life. The dimension of hope enables you to think a great deal about heaven, to sing about heaven, to long for it, to look forward to it. What a difference that makes, not only to the way you live but to the way you die, too. Hope is the anchor. It is the one thing that holds you when the world really gets you down. Life may be getting on top of you, and the world is so chaotic that you might think, "Where is it all going to? Will we ever get out of this trouble?" – but there is an anchor that holds you to the future, and it is the virtue of hope.

Paul thanks God for their faith and love, but as he writes this letter he is praying for them, to get their hope lifted a bit. That is why he's talking about predestination and the will of God. The will of God makes you hopeful – full of hope. It strengthens your grasp of the future. Your hope is strengthened by putting your trust in his will. If you look at your own will in the present, you are weak.

How many people have broken their New Year's resolution by January 9th – something you decided to do and you haven't quite made it. It depends whether you are given to New Year's resolutions. Isn't it disappointing to discover how weak-willed you are? But the will of God is what is the decisive factor here, and that is an anchor.

Now Paul prays for two things. First of all, an enlightened heart, the kind of understanding that comes from inside, not outside. Before a service begins, I pray for that for those to whom I preach. I pray that God would give the kind of understanding that doesn't come from me giving it to them, but from their understanding from inside: the eyes of the heart enlightened so that they can say, "I see", so that even when they are not in church listening they can have the spirit of wisdom and revelation in the knowledge of him. Not the knowledge of "it", the knowledge of *him*. That is the only knowledge worth having really, the knowledge of him, and that you may have the understanding that comes from inside. That understanding will at least bring you three things.

First of all, to understand the hope to which you were called, to understand where it is all heading. He who began a good work in you will complete it, and one day he is going to make you perfect in a perfect world. That is the hope to which you have been called—a hope of holiness, a hope of heaven. The eyes of your heart need to see this – that is what it is all heading up to reach. That is the target; that is the prize of the high calling; that is the aim, the goal of it all – that you may see this.

The second thing Paul wants them to see is how rich they are. We are millionaires. Behave as millionaires; look as if you are rich. Look as if somebody has given you a fortune, because you have received a fortune. That the eyes of your heart may be enlightened, that you may know what is the hope to which he has called you and what are the riches of his glorious inheritance in the saints. One day you will inherit the universe, it will all be yours and you will be able to move around it freely.

It seems pathetic to see man in his little machines trying to reach out a little step towards the stars. Doesn't it seem puny when you think of the riches of your inheritance? The whole universe will be yours to travel around in and explore. What an inheritance! "Blessed are the meek for they shall inherit the earth" – that would be a big enough inheritance, but to inherit a whole universe! Everything that is Christ's will come to you.

> A tent or a cottage, what do I care?
> They're building a palace for me over there.

That is the kind of song that helps a person to walk as a royal child, to behave as one – as rich beyond compare. That cures envy pretty quickly. You don't envy your neighbour whatever they have because they are going to lose it so quickly – and all that is waiting for you there.

The third thing he wants them to understand is the power available to us now, that you may understand the immeasurable greatness of his power. That phrase, "immeasurable greatness" – Paul would have been accused in those days of exaggeration. He is using Hollywood words. Think of "fabulous", "tremendous" – he is trying to get big words. "Great" – whatever the word you use today, put it in there instead of immeasurable greatness. It is the kind of exaggerated phrase that was used in those days loosely. But Paul means it: tremendous, immeasurable, fantastic greatness, that is what he is saying of the power, the might at work in us who believe – which God operates in us.

How big is God's power? At this point Paul takes off. He says it is the same power that lifted Jesus from the grave to highest heaven. You may have watched rockets taking off into space. The power! Thousands of gallons of liquid fuel burns in a second. The tremendous feeling – you can almost feel the earth under your feet shaking even though you are watching it on television. The power just to lift a man up a few miles! Think of the power that can raise a man from a cemetery to the throne of the universe. Christianity began among the dead—what a place to begin a religion!

Christianity began with a corpse—what a beginning! That cemetery might have been the end of everything. A cemetery is the end of all human achievement and the end of all human hopes, but it is the beginning of God's. Christianity really began in a garden tomb with a corpse. The mighty power of God says, "This is where the new creation is going to begin." He began by giving Christ a new body, and that is the beginning of the restoration of all things, the re-creation of the whole universe. His mighty power raised Jesus from the dead and brought him back to life. But it didn't stop there.

From the top of the Mount of Olives the mighty power of God went on raising Jesus up through the clouds, out into space, up, up, up. I don't know exactly where he is now; I know that he is in highest heaven. He is at the very highest point to which a man can be lifted, at the right hand of God the Father. He is above all power, and all rule, and all authority and dominion, so that everybody has to look up at Jesus now. There was a day when they looked down on him – even the angels looked down at the babe in Bethlehem.

Through his life he was despised and rejected of men and they looked down on him, and people looked at him on the cross – naked – and they laughed and they mocked. They looked down at Jesus all right. But now they have got to look up. If you are going to see Jesus, you have got to look right up as high as you can see, and your eyesight cannot go high enough to reach him. He is in the highest heaven now. This applies not only in time but in space; not only in this world, but in the world to come. He has been exalted. He is now the head of all things.

From the head, Paul immediately thinks of his feet. If his head is as high as that, where are his feet? The answer is: above all his enemies. Even to this day in certain primitive societies, when a battle is over, the victor stands on the defeated leaders who have to lie down on the ground, or else the victor will sit on a throne and his conquered enemies have to lie on the ground in front of the throne and he plants his feet on them. An ancient throne has been dug up by an archaeologist in Egypt. The throne has a footstool, and engraved on the footstool are portraits of all the enemies that king conquered, so that whenever he sat on his throne he could look down at his feet and look at his conquered foes.

That is the picture taken up here. He is the head over all things in highest heaven; his feet are on top of all his enemies. Where is his body? Here is the amazing thing: you are his body. Do you realise what that means? It means you are under the headship of Jesus, but you are on top of the enemies of Jesus. Satan, chief among them, is beneath the church. Because, if my anatomy is right, if you are the body you are above the feet and the feet are above the enemies. Do you see the picture as it develops? He is the head for the church, which is his body, and his feet have trampled down all his enemies. That makes the church more than conqueror. That makes you more than conqueror through him who loved you, and it means that the gates of Hades cannot prevail against the church.

Here are two amazing thoughts to close. He says he has been made head of all things for the church, which is his body, which completes him. Now that is the most bold and amazing statement. You – as the church – complete Christ; you fill Christ. Because now that he is exalted in highest heaven he needs a body on earth to go on doing his work down here. You complete Christ. You fill up Christ; you give him something he needs. So bold is that declaration that Paul is afraid we might get too big-headed about it and misunderstand it, so he says the church fills him, who fills all in all. We complete Christ, but Christ completes everything and everyone.

So we must never get too big for our shoes. We must

never think that because we are his body we are so terribly important, just as important as he is. It is he who completes us. We complete him who completes us; we fill him who fills everything.

Have you ever played with a telescope? I remember playing with one in a house we stayed in on one holiday—it was lying on the windowsill. I had great fun looking out to see the islands off the shore there through that old telescope – it brought them so near, gave you such a big view of things.

Then I did what I am sure you have done, I turned it round and looked the other way. Everything went so tiny and so far away. I think Paul is telling the Ephesians to get a bigger view of God – look at God through the right kind of telescope or through the right end of it. Don't get this small, far away view of God. Magnify the Lord with me! The word "magnify" means get a bigger view.

I want to contrast the difference between thinking in a small way about God and thinking in a big way. If you think in a small way you say, "God is now part of my plans." But if you think in a big way you say, "I am now part of God's plans." If you think in a small way you say, "There is a room in heaven for me." If you think in a big way you say, "There's going to be a Christian universe."

If you think in a small way you say, "I chose him." If you think in a big way you say, "He chose me." If you think in a small way you say, "Christ helps me." If you think in a big way you say, "Christ fills all in all." If you think in a small way you say, "I'd like to be comfortable, I'd like to be healthy, I'd like to be happy." But if you think in a big way you say, "I want to be whatever God wants me to be, and I need the spirit of wisdom and revelation and knowledge of him." That is a much bigger prayer.

If you think in a small way you say, "I wanted to be a Christian." If you think in a big way you say, "He wanted me to be his child." If you think in a small way you say, "We have received gifts from God." If you think in a big way you say, "We are gifts to God." Paul is teaching this: Get a bigger view, get the telescope right way around. See things from God's point of view and then you will live to the praise of his glory.

THE CHRISTIAN'S WORLD
– Redemption

Read Ephesians 2:1–10

A. SIN (1–3)

  1. Its CHARACTER – death
  2. Its CAUSE
       the world
       the devil
       the flesh
  3. Its CONSEQUENCE – wrath

B. SALVATION (4–10)

  1. Its CHARACTER – life
  2. Its CAUSE
       in mercy
       by grace
       through faith
  3. Its CONSEQUENCE – works

There are three questions that trouble the minds of every thinking man and woman. Question number one is: what is wrong with the world? There is something desperately wrong with it. You just need to listen to one news bulletin and you say, "There's something dreadfully wrong," and you hear many different answers. Some people say it is ignorance that lies at the root of it, others say it is poverty, others say oppression. People say, "Change the system – do this, that, and the other." What is wrong with the world?

The second question that occurs to you, if you think a little more deeply, is this: what is wrong with the people in it? For you very quickly come to the conclusion that this is where the problem lies—what's wrong with the people in the world? When you have thought that one through you come to the most disturbing question of all: what is wrong with *me*? Since I am one of the people in the world that has gone wrong.

John Wesley had a favourite little cliché which he was often quoting. He used to say, "Know your disease, know your cure." If there is something wrong with your body you will need a doctor and he will do three things: diagnosis, prognosis, prescription. Diagnosis means examining the symptoms to try and find their cause. Prognosis is deciding how serious the matter is going to be, where it is likely to lead, whether it is going to clear up of itself or whether it is very serious, needing medical or surgical help. Prescription is saying what help is going to relieve the need.

The Bible looks at the world problem, at the problem of the people in it, and at your problem, and it says your disease is sin. Not beating about the bush, the Bible keeps using that word. It doesn't use the word "vice" at all. I don't think it uses the word "crime" – or if it does, very little. It doesn't use the word "fault" a great deal—though all of us are conscious of our faults. The Bible cuts right through all this and says that the disease is sin. To make it a little more plain it also uses the word "trespass", which means to go where you are forbidden to go, to climb over a fence you should not have climbed. Sin is basically to break the laws of God, to disobey your conscience, to fall short of the life that God intended you to live—that is the disease, and it's a very personal one.

In the first few verses of chapter two, Paul goes through the diagnosis and the prognosis. He analyses the symptoms and the cause of those symptoms – how you got infected with this disease. He also makes a prognosis and tells you where it is likely to lead you. First of all, the symptom. How can you tell when a person has got sin? How can you tell that they have this disease? The answer is its character – its chief symptom is death. It makes a man dead. He may be living it up, he may be spending a lot of money, he may be doing a lot of exciting things, he may be travelling around all over the world, but as far as God is concerned, he is dead. He is a corpse spiritually. It is this spiritual deadness in people which tells us how widespread the disease is. You try to talk to someone about God and they are not interested. Talk about some sports personality and their eyes light up. Talk about Jesus Christ and you feel you have committed a faux pas. There is a deadness there, no spark of response. Spiritually, the disease of sin produces corpses and there are many corpses around.

What are the characteristics of a corpse? It is cold. Here is one of the symptoms of the disease of sin: people who are spiritually cold, no warmth about them in their worship. If they go to church it is a duty and they go through it but it is cold, not warm. Another characteristic of a corpse is that it is hard, not soft and tender as it once was. Another characteristic is that it is usually prone – it doesn't stand, doesn't walk, it just lies down. Above all, a corpse has decay, corruption in it, and will soon perish. Now that is the symptom.

In the parable of the prodigal son, when he came back home after – as the world would say – "really living it up", the father said, "This my son was dead, and he's alive again." Dead? While he was in the nightclubs of Antioch, dead? Yes, he was dead as far as God was concerned. God had no more from that man than you would get from a corpse. It is this spiritual death that is one of the most disturbing things when you try to spread the good news and you come up against death – people who seem incapable of responding. Don't be too hard on them for that. They are dead and they can't respond. Did you pray before you talked to them that God would give them a bit of life? Because unless he does they are incapable of responding to what you have to say to them. No wonder there is no response, they are dead.

Now how did people get this disease? What causes it? Where does the seat of infection come from? Paul gives us three sources of infection of this disease. The trouble is all of us have been in direct contact with all three and have picked up the disease from all three—the world, the devil, the flesh. Take the first – we were born into a world that was already infected by this disease. We breathed it in, we lived among people with the disease, we mixed with them—that's the way to catch things.

The world in which we live is a world that is spiritually dead, and we became dead because we came into a dead world. We came into a world that is a sinful one. It is our environment and you can test this: we don't like being different so as we grew up we conformed to that world in many different ways. But watch young people and see the pressure on them to conform to their class at school, to conform to their friends, to fit in to the world in which they have been born. The pressure to follow the world is terribly strong and very hard to resist. In fact, none of us has been able to resist it fully.

So the world was one source of infection, but the second source was the devil. Who is actually the leader of this world? Who is in charge of it? Who is running it? Sometimes you feel nobody is, it is so chaotic. Then at other times you see how evil is so well organised, so international, so powerful, that you come to the conclusion that somebody is responsible. Men and women are looking around for someone to blame, they are trying to find someone you can say is behind it all. Who is really behind it? The answer is, according to this: the prince of the power of the air. What a title to give the devil: prince, power, air. It is as much as to say that the devil's domain is the atmosphere – that is where he holds sway. As long as you breathe the air, you are breathing in the atmosphere of Satan. As long as you breathe you are within his power, his dominion. The only way out of it is to stop breathing. People say, "Well, I can get into a space machine and get out of it." Can you? You will take with you the same air; you are still a breathing animal. He is the prince. Jesus called him the prince of this world; the ruler of this world, and Paul called him the god of this world. Make no mistake about it as to who is behind it all. You are not only born into an infected environment, you are born into a dominion ruled over by someone whose ambition it is to make you sin, and he is more subtle and powerful than you are.

As if two sources of infection were not enough there is a third, which Paul calls the flesh. Now what does he mean by that? Just the body? No, he includes the brain in that, the mind as well as the body, and goes on to talk about the mind and the body. For the word "flesh" in the Bible doesn't just mean your physical body, it means everything you inherited when you were born. It is not just your environment that is the problem, it is your heredity. My wife and I passed on to our children a nature of flesh. It is one of the most disturbing things about having children. Having a meal with one family, I said, "Does your little girl say anything yet?" Their first reply was, "She's learned to say no."

How very early, even before a baby talks, self-will appears – and it did in you, so don't think the next generation is worse than you were. Why is this? It is because the body and the brain we are born with are already part of this fallen world. The "flesh" means that we are not only struggling with an environment outside us and a devil outside us but with cravings, affections, ideas and desires within ourselves, and every one of us has this struggle.

So the infection has come from three sources. What then is the prognosis? How serious a condition is it? Can we say, "Well, it's a general condition, and a lot of people have it, and it will clear up, and there is nothing much to worry about"? People do say this. They say, "Well, no one's perfect. Everybody's got their faults, it's not too serious." Is that a good prognosis? The prognosis of Paul is that you have a killer disease – it is a killer and without radical treatment you are a dead man, and you will be dead forever through it. Or, as Paul puts it, and I must explain his phrase, "You are by nature children of wrath." Now the word "wrath" means anger. It means that because you are what you are you stand under the dark thundercloud of God's anger.

You may not realise that, and he doesn't show it too fully at the moment. He does show it in some ways – he shows it by taking the brakes off your life. If men give God up, he gives men up and says, "All right, do what you want and see what happens." That is one way he shows his wrath. But the Bible talks about a *day* of wrath, meaning a day when everybody will experience God's anger for having sinned. That day will be the most dreadful day people have ever had. It is bad enough when you see somebody in your family really angry with you. Think back to your childhood when a parent was angry with you – was it not a dreadful experience? If they had just cause to be, that was dreadful. There is coming a day when God will be angry and show it, and show it very severely.

Bunyan's book *The Pilgrim's Progress* begins with a man who has a great burden on his back. It is a burden that is getting bigger every day because he has started reading his Bible and he knows that he has sinned and that one day he is going to face God in his anger. He is bowed down and wandering around outside a city saying, "I know the city's going to be destroyed, I know I'm going to be. What can I do?" A man called Mr. Evangelist meets him and gives him a little sheet of paper. Written on it are these words: "Flee from the wrath to come" – get your problem dealt with, get rid of that burden on your back before the anger comes.

That is the beginning of the Christian life, when you realise that the prognosis is wrath. Now that is the black side, but you don't understand the light until you have seen the darkness clearly. You don't understand the glory of the gospel until you have seen the terror of it. The gospel is bad news before it is good news. You don't understand how good the good news is until you understand how bad the bad news is.

So the gospel is for dead, hopeless people who are facing nothing but the wrath of God in the future, and it is good news. What is the good news? The good news is that where men can do nothing about sin whatever, except hide it and disguise it for a time, God can deal with it, and there is a cure. Here comes the prescription.

First, the character of the cure is *life*, as the character of the disease is death: you has he made alive when you were dead. That is the good news. It is good news for spiritually dead people that they can be made alive. There was a time when you were spiritually dead – you could go to a church service and nothing happened in you. You might as well have been a corpse for all the good it did you. Then there came a day when life began, you began to realise there was something in it. Like a germinating seed, you began to reach up to the sunlight of God's love, you responded, there was life, and it was God who made you alive when you were dead.

It is a miracle of resurrection that is needed. You will never save a person by education or by reformation. You will never save someone through politics or science. There is no military cure for the problems of the world because all these answers assume that man is alive, and that you are dealing with a live man. But of course you can't save a man that way because he is dead, and that requires a miracle of resurrection, and only God can do that. He did it with Jesus; he has done it with us. You has he made alive together with Christ – he was the first to be raised from the dead and now we follow.

So Paul says the cure is this: "You has he quickened." That means to make a corpse live. Suddenly, you begin to see things you never saw before, you begin to hear God speaking to you. You never heard him before. You begin to talk and he makes the dumb to speak and you begin to start talking to God as someone you know – not just saying prayers in the hope that someone might listen, but you are talking to someone you know. The deaf begin to hear. A corpse can't hear, a corpse can't speak, a corpse can't see, but he made you alive, and you now respond to him.

"He raised you," says Paul, "as he raised Christ." Now how high did he raise you? The answer is as far as he raised Christ he has already raised you. He not only brought Christ back to earth, but he lifted him up through space to the highest heaven and made him to sit at the right hand of God the Father, in the heavenly places. If, when preaching, I ask you, "Where are you sitting?" – then if you are a Christian you can say, "In heaven." Your body may be sitting on a hard wooden pew, but that is only a body – it is not the "you". Your body is on the way out anyway.

You are sitting in the heavenly places in Christ Jesus – that is where you sit "in Christ". You are already out of the dominion of the devil. Your body is still here and that is why he gets you through the flesh, through your body and your brain. But your spirit is already where one day a new body will join it in the heavenly places in Christ Jesus.

That is the answer to your problem, to the problem of the people in the world, and therefore the problem of the world itself – to get out of the world and into heaven now, and get away from the prince of the power of the air now. That is the character of the new life – life as opposed to death.

How do you get that? There were three sources from which you got your sin. Now there are three big words and three little words from which you get your life. The three big words are mercy, grace, and faith. The three little words are "in" mercy, "by" grace, "through" faith. The little words in the Bible are as important as the big words because they are the words of God. Those little prepositions are all important – we are not saved by faith—faith can't save you. We are saved by grace through faith.

Let us start with the first big and little word, "God, being rich in mercy...." In fact, I should have stopped at one little word at the beginning of v. 4: "but". That little word makes the whole difference. It is as if a doctor said to you, "I'm sorry, you've got something very serious, *but* there is now a cure." That little "but" would mean everything to you. "Did he say *but*?" "But God, being rich in mercy..." – and "in mercy" means that God loves to give people what they do not deserve. That is what the word mercy means: you don't deserve it but you will have it. If God only had justice, I haven't a chance. If God only has fairness, I haven't a chance. But God, being rich in mercy, loves to help the undeserving and that includes all of us.

The second big word and little word is "by grace". Somebody has said that this is the most offensive thing in the Christian gospel, and it is. It means that you will never get the cure through anything you have done. This is particularly an issue in Britain where there was once a man called Pelagius who taught a version of Christianity which has been called ever since Pelagianism. It was one of the heresies that got into Christianity in this country. Quite frankly, it is still around: basically, in very simple terms, if you do good you will get to heaven. That is such a common idea. You will hear it mentioned at most funerals outside the Christian faith. "Well, if ever anybody deserved to get there, he did," says a relative or friend, thinking he did good. This is one of the greatest difficulties you have in preaching the gospel: people believe that they have done enough good to get there. If we did good deeds every day of our life, it wouldn't get us an inch nearer heaven, and that is what grace means. It means two things quite simply: the good deeds you have done cannot help you to be cured and the bad deeds you have done need not hinder you being cured.

That means what is most offensive to those who have tried to be good: that a thoroughly bad character can get to heaven by grace. A dying thief on a cross can step into glory. That is offensive. Why should he have salvation when I have tried to do good all my life and tried to live decently? That is the inherent pride that we have. The expression "by grace" means it is God's free gift – it is all his generosity, his doing. There is nothing you can do to help yourself, but he will save you and get you there by grace.

Not of works, lest any man should boast—that is what

God doesn't like. God won't have anyone in heaven saying, "Well, I got here under my own steam you know." Nor will he even have a man saying, "Well, I half saved myself and God forgave the rest." For then somebody else can say, "Well, I three quarters saved myself and he only needed to forgive a quarter." Boasting is the fundamental sin of pride. God says, "I won't have it in heaven. You all come on the same basis. I bring you, I save you, I give it to you, so that there is no boasting and nobody ever thinks they are better than another." That is what cures pride in a Christian fellowship. We all know deep down that none of us is better than another and that none of us has any more right to be here than anyone else, whatever kind of a life we have tried to live. We are here by grace.

But the third thing is this: "through faith". A gift has to be received. You can't give a gift to someone if they won't take it. Some people won't accept a gift. It has been estimated that there are thousands upon thousands of people in this country who could receive financial help from official sources but who won't take it. It is one of the problems that they call it charity and refuse it when it is there to help. The country wants people to have help who need it. You can't give a gift unless it is received. The only thing you contribute to your salvation is to stretch out a hand and take it, and that is what is called faith. You are not saved *by* faith, you are saved *through* faith – believing that it is for you and taking it, that's all.

Now there is one final thing to be said. If I stopped at this point, and if Paul stopped at this point, there would be a most important thing missed out. For if you do not need good deeds before you begin to be saved it is very easy to drop into the error of thinking that you do not need them afterwards. In other words, whenever you preach the gospel of grace and say you don't need to do good deeds to be saved, there are always going to be some who jump to the wrong conclusion and say, "Then it doesn't matter how we live. As long as I believe, I can do bad deeds. As long as I believe, it doesn't matter. I don't need to help anybody else. I'm on my way to glory, hallelujah, that's all there is to it." But that is not what God intended.

For now comes another little important word, we are saved in mercy, by grace, through faith *for good works*. Do you notice that in v. 10? "For good works" – created in Christ Jesus for good works. You are not saved *by* good deeds but you are saved *for* good deeds. Do you understand that there is a whole world of difference? No longer am I saying, "I am doing good in order to get to heaven," I am now saying, "I am doing good because I am going to heaven." What a big incentive to do good – to start living right down here the kind of life you'll be living up there, of service and doing good.

There are two big differences between an unbeliever doing a good deed and a believer doing a good deed – profound differences which make the good deeds quite different from each other. Firstly, we are his workmanship. In other words, the good deed springs from a good deed of God. He has already worked on us so that we can work for others. In other words, it springs from a person whose been changed by God, and that makes a big difference. We are his workmanship – he has already done a good work in us so now we do good works for others. Do you see the first difference? An unbeliever can do good deeds—Jesus admitted that. He said, "If you then being evil know how to give good gifts to your children...." Yes, the unbeliever can do good deeds, and can do it without letting God remake their life. Therefore that is why, in the last analysis, when they face God, as far as they are concerned they are no better off than if they had not done those good deeds. Other people have benefitted, but they haven't because they have not allowed God to do his good deed in them before they have done good deeds for others.

The other difference between Christian good deeds and others' good deeds is this: "...created in Christ Jesus for good works, which God has prepared beforehand that we should walk in them." In other words, the good deeds that a Christian does are those that God planned for him or her to do. He asks God first, "What good deed do you want me to do?" Otherwise it may be a good deed that he did not want you to do or it may be just a good deed that you thought of doing. God has planned your good deeds. There are certain things he wants you to do that are good deeds. Your good deeds for others are going to meet a much wider range of needs. Before you are a Christian you can meet physical needs and emotional needs, and even mental needs, but you can't meet spiritual needs. Your neighbour's spiritual needs can't be met and the one good deed that God wants you to do for someone else more than any other is the good deed of telling them about Jesus. That is a good deed that he has planned for you to do and now you can.

From this passage a line goes straight through the human race. There is no grading, nor a spectrum of different colours, there are only two categories of people in the whole world: dead and alive – and there is nothing in between. There are no half-deads. You, when you were dead in trespasses and sins, he has made alive. You are either dead or alive. You are either outside of Christ and living on earth – in the air over which the devil has control – or you are sitting in heavenly places in Christ Jesus. There is no in-between. Everyone in a congregation is one or the other. You are either dead with a disease that is a killer and that will one day bring you under the wrath of God, or you are alive and you are created for good works and you are already sitting in heavenly places where your body will one day join your spirit.

THE CHRISTIAN'S WORLD
– Reconciliation

Read Ephesians 2:11–22

A. DISUNITY IN THE FLESH (11–12)

  1. ALIENS –
      the Christ
      the commonwealth
      the covenant

  2. ATHEISTS –
      the confidence
      the Creator

B. UNITY IN THE SPIRIT (13–22)

  1. One BLOOD – acceptance with God
  2. One BODY – access to God
  3. One BUILDING – accommodation for God

Many years ago, my wife and I were in Gibraltar, staying in my brother-in-law's flat, just about twenty yards from the border between Gibraltar and Spain, a border that had been closed tight for some months. There was a no-man's land of about fifty yards between two lines of barbed wire. Either side of these frontiers we saw little groups of people with binoculars waving to each other. They could not meet, they could not talk – so near and yet so far. All they could do was to look at each other through binoculars. I had seen that twice before. I had seen it in Berlin, and I will never forget the horror with which one saw that line of concrete blocks, so crudely built, with the step ladders either side for relatives to wave at each other across a man-made barrier. I saw it in Jerusalem before the Six-day War, and looked across no-man's land from Jewish territory to Arab territory.

There have been many divisions in the human race. Our world is full of divisions and demilitarised zones, and we go on dividing each other up. But two thousand years ago the very deepest division there has ever been was the thing that filled out the horizon of the thoughts of the man who wrote this letter to the Ephesians. That division was between Jew and Gentile. For alone among all divisions that have divided people, this one came from God, whilst all the others have been man-made. That God made it means it was deeper than any other distinction and may go a long way to explaining the emotions that have centred on this division.

Indeed, the long history of anti-Semitism has had its counterpart in the Jewish attitude to the Gentiles also. This very deep division was the largest gulf that Paul ever knew. He had been born on one side of that gulf. He was a Hebrew of the Hebrews, a Pharisee of the Pharisees. Claiming descent from the most exclusive tribe of all, the little tribe of

Benjamin, and named after the first king of Israel who came from that tribe, Saul grew up to be proud that he was on the right side of that gulf. Being a Pharisee, if he had brushed up against a Gentile in the marketplace his reaction would have been to go home and have a bath. He is now writing a letter that is going to cross that gulf – he is writing to Gentiles and that in itself is a miracle.

Before he became a Christian he would never have thought of sitting down and writing a letter to those on the other side of the gulf, especially a letter in terms of love like this. It is a miracle—something has happened. I have said the gulf has been bridged, but I think it is truer to put it in his words: the middle wall of partition had gone down, smashed. It is the story of that which we are going to explore now – that Christ has bridged the deepest gulf or smashed the highest barrier that existed between people. In Christ we have our hope for the unity between every kindred, tribe, tongue and people. If Christ can bring Jew and Gentile together, he can bring anyone together. That is the gospel of peace that we can preach to those who are near and to those who are afar off.

Paul, writing as a Jew to Gentiles, doesn't avoid any uncomfortable thoughts that he had. He told them exactly where they were. He is saying: I was born on the right side of the gulf, but you were most certainly on the wrong side of it. Outside of Christ you were so disunited from us that you were disconnected from God. For God has chosen to work through one nation toward the others.

I suppose that God could have put on the earth different nations and then spoken to each one and sent an American messiah, and a British messiah, and a Russian messiah, and a Jewish messiah. But he didn't do that. In his own wisdom, for some reason he said, "I am going to send a Messiah to the Jews and through them all the nations of the earth will be blessed."

It is as if with our children when they were young I had got some sweets for them and I could do one of two things. I could have given each of them a sweet or I could give one of them the bag and say, "Go and share that with the others." The second method does more for family life than the first. If you are creating a family, that is one of the little things you could do. If ever you want to see an apple perfectly cut in half then say to two children, "One of you cut it in half and the other has first pick."

God, in his mercy, wanted a family. So in his wisdom he said to the Jews: I give you a Messiah. I give you the promises. I give you the scriptures. I give you the covenant. I give you the commonwealth. I give it all to you, now it has got to be shared. One of the tragedies of their history is that they did not learn to share it as God intended them to do, but when Christ came that was put right.

Let us look at our position as Gentiles outside of Christ. It is a pretty rough picture – we are hopeless. We haven't an earthly hope of getting through to God. We are Gentiles. What have we got? Nothing. We are on the wrong side of the great divide in the human race. Paul describes Gentiles outside of Christ with two words: "aliens" and "atheists". We have tended in our narrow-mindedness to think of the Jew as an alien wherever he has been. This is really the deep-rooted, uncomfortable relationship that has existed wherever the Jews have gone. They have been felt to be strangers, sojourners, misfits, aliens who don't really belong. The truth is that in fact it is the Gentiles who don't really belong, not the Jews. It is the Gentiles who are aliens. We are the strangers, we are the sojourners, we are the ones just passing through with no final home.

When we look at the dispersed people of God who had no home for nearly two thousand years, it is we who have had no home. So Paul says, "You were aliens, remember this.

You had no Christ." The word "Christ" is a Greek word, but it is a translation of the Hebrew word "Messiah". It is a Jewish idea and we would never have used the word but for the Jews. It is not a word that has sprung up elsewhere; it is not a hope that other nations have. People may have put their hopes in human deliverers, human politicians, but this nation for the last three thousand years has looked for an anointed one from God. The word "Christ" means anointed. That is why in the coronation service of Queen Elizabeth II, oil was put on her forehead and it was called the "chrism" – the anointing. So the Hebrew people looked for an anointed one from God. The tragedy is that the majority of them are still looking and he has been. But that has been their hope.

Here is a word we are using all the time in our worship but I wonder how much content we give to it. You see, because we haven't been hoping for centuries for the Christ, the word "Christ" is no more to us than a title, a name. We don't get all excited about that word. But someone with the Hebrew hope of the Messiah who is told that Jesus is the Messiah — their heart begins to beat, "The Christ?" Remember how, in the early days of Jesus' earthly life, one person would go to another and say, "We've found the Christ." Been waiting for thirty generations; we've found him! The excitement of the word "Christ"! But Gentiles were separated from Christ.

Gentiles, you had no commonwealth! There is only one citizenship that is permanent in this world, and that is the citizenship of Israel. It is the only nation that will survive all the way through. We were strangers to the commonwealth of Israel. And no covenant – that is a word that we Gentiles have got to get used to. The very word "covenant" implies a marriage, a close relationship, a covenant with God that carries certain of God's promises with it. The Bible is stacked with promises, over four thousand of them I am told, though I would think it might even be more. But to whom were those promises given? Until Christ came they were given to the Hebrew people, those within the covenant, those married to God. The promises made to Abraham, Isaac, Jacob and to Moses were promises to the nation of Israel. As Gentiles none of it was ours.

Not only were we aliens, but we have already got to the point where we can say the second word: "atheists". Now what is an atheist? We tend to use the word with a wrong meaning. We say a man is an atheist if he doesn't believe there is a God. I suppose if that is the meaning of the word "atheist" there are few real atheists. There are more who are agnostic. But, according to the Bible, every Gentile is an atheist. The only time the word "atheists" is used in the Bible is in this passage in Ephesians (see 2:12). This is where we get the word "atheist" from. Paul, writing in Greek, uses the word *atheoi*. You Gentiles were *atheoi*. The word *theos* means God. The little prefix "a" means without. You can believe there is a God and spend all of next week without him – that is being one of the *atheoi*. You can have plenty of religion and be without God. You can have your temples, and your shrines, your daily prayers, your sacrifices, and you can be without God. According to Paul, even in spite of all the religion in the world, Gentiles are *atheoi*, without God, because God is the God of the Jew.

Therefore because they have no God, no Father in heaven, Gentiles are also without a future, without a hope. They have nothing to look forward to except the grave. Philips translates this verse (v. 12) like this and I think this is a very good translation, "Remember you had nothing to look forward to and no God to whom you could turn." That's what the Gentile condition is, and I was born a Gentile. I am a Gentile in the flesh; I am a Gentile in the world, and those two phrases sum up the Gentile's position and address. A Gentile is in the flesh and in the world and therefore he has no Christ, no citizenship, no covenant, no future and no Father in heaven. If you are a Gentile, that would have been your lot if Christ had never come.

But look at v. 13, the first word, underline it. There is a "but" in the middle. "But" as soon as you cease to be in the flesh and in the world and are in Christ Jesus the whole picture is changed. Now you are on the right side of the great divide because you are in a Jew. You are now in Christ Jesus and he was a Jew, so now everything is yours in him. You have stepped over the gulf. You are now in Christ Jesus, and what a difference that makes. We are going to look at that difference now.

From a disunited mankind, separated by barriers, walls, barbed wire, stone fences there is now one new humanity in Christ Jesus. This fellowship crosses Jew and Gentile frontiers. I think that is lovely – all one in Christ Jesus. Though whenever I meet a Hebrew Christian I must admit envy smites my heart. I would love to be what I think is a normal Christian—to have had all that history, to have had all that in your bones from the beginning, and then to discover the Messiah. What a thrill that must be. It's a thrill I could never have. But God in his mercy has taken a poor Gentile and grafted him into the stock of Israel.

Look what happens now. Paul changes from the word "you" to the words "we" and "our". Here is a Jew writing to Gentiles, talking about "us". Again and again he uses the word "one". I pick up three ideas here: one blood, one body, one building. Get the feel of the picture language, get right into it: Jew and Gentile are now one blood.

Do you know why the Jew didn't like the Samaritan? Because the Samaritan was only half a Jew. In the old days there were Jews and Gentiles, but some of them intermarried and the result was a Samaritan, a kind of semi-Jew, mixed blood. The true Jew valued his true Hebrew blood so much that he would not have anything to do even with a half-caste Jew. So much did he think of his blood, the blood that had coursed through his veins from way back, he kept his family tree carefully, "My blood is Hebrew blood. I'm true Jewish blood." That was one meaning of the word "blood" to the Jew.

The other was not just the blood inside him, but the blood outside him — the blood that had been sprinkled on him, the blood of the sacrifices that God gave his people. The word "blood" meant a great deal to the Jew and that is why it appears very often in the Old Testament. But what is Paul talking about now? He is talking about the blood of Jesus. That, in his thinking, has replaced the other two meanings of the word "blood" for him. He is not concerned now whether a man has Jewish blood or Gentile blood going through his veins. He is not concerned now about the blood of Jewish sacrifices. He is concerned about only one thing — that the blood of Jesus, the one perfect and sufficient sacrifice for the sins of the whole world, is now in the hearts of Jew and Gentile. Through the blood of the cross Jesus has made peace, harmony, between Jew and Gentile.

Gentile and Jewish believers in Jesus are of *one blood*, the blood of Jesus Christ is in the hearts of both. That makes us brothers and sisters. When you come to God through Christ you have not only come to a Father, you have come to a family of brothers and sisters. You are one blood, and every time you take the cup and drink the wine at the Lord's Supper you remember that you are one blood in him. How did that come about?

Here is an interesting thing. Paul tells us that Christ in his flesh on the cross abolished those things that made Jews different from us. Circumcision was one of them – that is abolished now; other laws, ceremonial, ritual laws, many of the laws, for Christ has abolished the law of commandments and ordinances. That is what made the Jew a Jew in the sense of his behaviour. That is what made him different from others. He kept the Saturday as the Sabbath, he circumcised his boy children. All this rigmarole that he went through, which God had given to him, is abolished. So the Jew, in a sense the Jewish system, has been abolished. Christ has made the Jew like the Christian now. Indeed, we are no longer under the Jewish law.

Now some people could say, "Well, that is a dangerous thing to do, to abolish all the law, because some of the law – well, there was good moral guidance and commandments in that law. Do you mean we are finished with the Ten Commandments?" Let me put it this way: if Christ has abolished everything that made the Jew Jewish, what has he replaced that with? The answer is *himself*. There was a film *Martin Luther* with a very telling scene, in which the father superior of the monastery where Luther was a monk said to him, "I hear you want to abolish all the aids to Catholic devotion – that you want to abolish images, relics, praying to the saints, all our observances. If you take these away what are you going to put in their place?" Luther replies, "Jesus Christ, man only needs Jesus Christ."

He is now our law. He will now give us the moral guidance. If he repeats one of the Ten Commandments we accept it, not because it is one of the Ten Commandments but because Christ has repeated it, and Christ has laid that law upon us. It is a law of liberty that springs from a personal relationship. Oh yes, the moral standards of God have not changed, but we accept them from Christ. He has abolished the law and replaced it with himself, abolished in his flesh the law of commandments and ordinances written against us – and now we have Christ. That is what has made Jew and Gentile one. So a Jewish believer in Jesus with their Jewish traditions and David Pawson with his Gentile traditions –

neither of us bring those traditions to the other now. We offer Christ, one blood.

The second picture here is *one body*. You can't have a greater picture of unity than one body – just one. Paul talks about one body in two senses. The one body of Christ that was put on a cross, that was smashed – his flesh has created one new body. We are one body, we are not separate people. We are one body in Christ Jesus. Now Gentiles in Christ are even closer to God than the Jews outside Christ are. That is an amazing thing. They have actually become part of his body.

Jew and Gentile are now one body and we both have access to God in one Spirit. For a body must have a spirit in it to live. The one body that we now are has one Spirit in it, and in that one Spirit we can come right through to the Father. When Jesus died, even the veil of the temple was ripped in two. We have access right into the holy of holies. You can't get closer to God than in one Spirit, and in the Spirit you get very near, nearer than even the Jews could get in the days of the temple.

Which brings us to the final thought: *one building*. I have seen a lovely model on a hillside of the magnificent temple, and there you see the middle wall. There was a court of the Gentiles but then the notice: on penalty of death, no Gentile.

So if you were a poor Gentile seeking God you had to make a long journey to the Jewish land and you had to go to a Jewish temple, and you could go in the outside yard. It was that court that got filled up with money changers and people buying and selling animals. It was into that court that Jesus came and he said, "How dare you do this! Don't you know that this was meant to be a house of prayer for all the Gentiles, for all the nations? And look what you've done, you've filled up the only place where they can pray to my Father with merchandise. Get out" – and he whipped them out. But even he didn't take a Gentile further than the next gate because he hadn't died yet. But when he died, that next gate became obsolete and now Gentiles can come right in to the holy of holies with Jews, and the middle wall is gone.

Forty years after Jesus died, that physical wall was still standing. But it was wrecked by the Romans in AD 70 and it has never been rebuilt. Do you know that Paul wrote this letter to the Ephesians about eight years before that middle wall was actually destroyed? He didn't know it was going to be. Do you know that shortly after he wrote this letter he was going to be arrested and sent to Rome as a prisoner? Do you know why they arrested Paul? He was accused of taking a Gentile through that gate, a man called Trophimus. They started to say around the temple, "This man took a Gentile into the Jewish court in the temple." It was a false charge; he had done no such thing. But in fact he had. He had brought thousands of Gentiles through that gate, not through the building, but through to God. His whole ministry had been bringing Gentiles through the middle wall of partition. Paul had two emotions in him when he wrote to Gentiles. One was how glad he was that the Gentiles were now right in. The other was how sad he was that so many of his own fellow citizens were right out. The simple fact is now that believing Jews and believing Gentiles are one on one side of the gulf, and unbelieving Jews and unbelieving Gentiles are on the other side of the gulf. The division is another way now.

Let me get back to one building. Paul realised that God had made the old temple, of stone and timber and gold, obsolete. Where was God going to live on earth now? Where would his presence be found now? Then Paul saw it. The Holy Spirit revealed to him that out of Jew and Gentile God was building one building. On the foundation of prophets and apostles, with Jesus Christ as the great cornerstone holding the walls together, the Jew and Gentile were being built together into a building, a habitation fitly framed together, a temple for God to inhabit by his Spirit.

You, whether you be Jew or Gentile, if you are in Christ, you are being built into a holy temple and there is no wall of partition in it – none at all. God by his Spirit dwells in this temple. One blood, one body, one building. The deepest division of the human race has vanished. In Christ, therefore, every other division can go. I have a vision of the church where there is no distinction whatsoever. I was once asked to go to be a minister in a church in another country. I made inquiries about the church and I was told that I would have to conduct a service for black people at nine and for white people at eleven. I could not go.

In Christ there is no wall of partition. We hear much about the generation gap – that the young must worship God their way and the old their way, and never the two shall meet, and we must just stay in our own types of worship. That is a lie. The church is to be for young and old. All our cultural differences, all our traditions, they fall before the Lord Jesus Christ. I see a church in which people of different colour, different class and different culture become one building, one body.

I emphasise that the cross is the key to this whole passage. If the cross and the blood of Christ on that cross is what brought this new unity, it has also brought this new division. For the deepest division among mankind now is not between east and west, or between black and white, or rich and poor, or young and old. The biggest difference is the difference between those who believe and those who do not believe. You are no longer on the wrong side of the gulf because you are a Gentile. You are on the wrong side if you are an unbeliever. If you are a believer you are one with every other believer, be they Jew or Gentile.

THE CHRISTIAN'S WISDOM

Read Ephesians 3

A. MYSTERY OF THE GENTILES (1–6)
 1. Its communication (1–5)
        a. Prisoner
        b. Steward
        c. Apostle
 2. Its content (6)
        a. Fellow-heirs
        b. Members
        c. Partakers

B. MINISTRY OF THE GOSPEL (7–21)
 1. The preacher (7–8)
        a. The gift
        b. The grace
 2. The plan (9–10)
        a. Hidden in the Creator
        b. Revealed through the church
        c. Observed by the angels
 3. The purpose (11–12)
        a. Fact of Christ
        b. Faith of Christians
 4. The price (13)
        a. What
        b. Why
 5. The prayer (14–19)
        a. Strengthened
        b. Indwelt
        c. Established
        d. Enlarged
        e. Filled
 6. The power (20–21)
        a. His greatness
        b. His glory

When God does a new thing he chooses the most unlikely people to do it. We would choose someone suited to the task; God seems to go to the most unsuitable person and tell them to do it. For example, in the eighteenth century, when he wanted to reach the smugglers of Cornwall, and the hard living, hard fighting miners of Bristol, he went to Oxford and took hold of a scholar from one of the colleges and sent him down to those places. His name: John Wesley. You and I wouldn't have chosen that man to reach those people. God has been sending Western missionaries overseas for a long time. Now he is sending missionaries from developing countries to England to win people for Christ. I remember a man who was very hard, and man after man tried to win him for Christ and they couldn't get through. They thought the only person who could win him was a real man's man. But one day a little nine-year-old girl climbed on his knee and said, "Daddy, why don't you come to God?" She got through.

When God wanted to bring in the Gentiles, those outside the pale as far as Jews were concerned, he went for the most fanatical Jew he could lay his hands on, a man called Saul of Tarsus. A Pharisee of the Pharisees, a man who wouldn't sit at the same table with a Gentile, and God arrested him when he was on his way to arrest them. He had letters to put people in prison. Later, giving his testimony, he said, "On my way to arrest the Christians, Christ apprehended me, arrested me."

He was in custody for ever afterwards. He was a "prisoner of the Lord Jesus Christ" – that is how he described himself. It meant that one day he would be a prisoner of someone else too. As you read this letter, you can hear the chains clanking as he moves his pen. Many great books have come out of prison when Christians have been locked up for their faith. Now here is the most Jewish Jew of all, and yet he says, "To me God told his great secret," and he has a tremendous sense of bursting to share the secret. How are you with secrets? I'm sure you like being told one. Can you keep it? There is only one joy greater than being told a secret and that is passing it on to someone else, and this is how Paul felt. I remember the day that Cliff Richard was coming to our house for tea and we told the children and said, "But you must keep it a secret till after he's been." They were thrilled to share the secret, but my, they were bursting to tell it. They found on the Monday when they got to school and told it that there were many who wouldn't even believe it was true, as Paul found when he shared God's great secret. But this is what he says, "I Paul..." and even the name that he uses is interesting. His parents never called him Paul, they called him Saul, after the first king of Israel who came from the little tribe of Benjamin from which Saul of Tarsus came. When the word "Saul" is put into the Greek language it becomes "Paul". Here is a man who is prepared to change his name from a Jewish name to a Gentile name, and the change is astonishing.

First of all, in this chapter he talks about being a prisoner for the Gentiles, and a steward of God's grace. What does the word "steward" mean to you? Someone who gives out hymn books at the door of a church? In the north, where I come from, when we worked on the farm we were always under a steward. I was responsible to the farm steward. There were fourteen of us working on the farm. There was a farmer who owned the farm, but he owned quite a few so we didn't see all that much of him. The steward was the manager, the one responsible for looking after the farm and presenting the profits to him. That is what a steward is, a manager of someone else's property. Paul says, "I'm a prisoner and I'm a steward. I manage God's grace. I'm a steward of God's generosity. He's put me in charge of distributing his wealth." What a wonderful task! Supposing somebody gave you a cheque for a million pounds and said, "You go and give that away to others, those in need," wouldn't you be thrilled? Wouldn't you long to go and visit someone and say, "Here, I've got a gift for you." A steward of God's grace – that indeed is the highest privilege a person could have. To have all the wealth of God, and God says, "Now go and share it with other people; go and distribute it to those in need."

You can do that wherever you are. You can do that in chains. You may be in a prison cell. You can still be a steward of God's grace. Think of the soldiers who were chained to Paul. Fancy being chained to Paul for hours on end! Can you imagine it? We know later in the chapter that when he said his prayers he got on his knees. The centurion would have to stand there with the chain down to this man on his knees, and we know that Paul prayed aloud when he prayed. Can you imagine being chained to a missionary for hours on end? They just wouldn't have a chance. That is why Paul is able to write in his letters, "Those of Caesar's household salute you." You can be a steward of God's grace wherever you are, in whatever circumstances.

Now let us come to the secret: Paul calls it a "mystery", and that word doesn't mean quite the same thing to us today. A mystery thriller means something that is puzzling, mysterious, but something that will be sorted out before the end of the novel, and that is partly the meaning here, but I think we could better translate it "secret", God's secret, which can now be told. When I joined the Royal Air Force and was commissioned as an officer I had to make myself familiar with the Official Secrets Act. I had to promise that for twenty-five years after certain things happened I would not divulge them, and then they could be told, and the secret could be shared. Then you can write your memoirs, produce your war novels, and all the rest. That is why a spate of World War II novels were published when we were past the period of official secrets. God had an official secret and he kept it for generations. He didn't tell people about it. It isn't anywhere to be found in the Old Testament. He kept it all the way through the history of the Jews and then he shared it. He told it to the apostles and the prophets of the New Testament. He told it to Peter first, then he told it to Paul. He told it to the other apostles and the prophets. It was shared and now it is out of the bag. What is the secret? The secret is that Gentiles can now come to God apart from the Jews.

If you read the Old Testament, you find the Gentiles are mentioned again and again, but every time they are mentioned as coming to the Jews to find God. To Abraham: "In you and in your seed shall all the nations of the earth be blessed" – for centuries people took that to mean that others could come and share the blessings, but they would have to come to Abraham and his descendants. You find there are prophecies of all the nations seeking God – but how? By saying, "Come, let us go up to the mountain of the Lord, to Jerusalem, and there find God." This is the plan for the Gentiles revealed in the Old Testament. To Peter, and then to Paul, and then to the other apostles, God reveals: I am going to share my secret with you; I am going to turn to the Gentiles, and I'm going to deal with them direct.

What a secret! It meant that a person who sought God did not need to join Israel, did not need to be circumcised, did not need to keep the Ten Commandments; they could come straight to God through Jesus. For now that Jesus was the seed of Abraham, that is all the seed of Abraham a Gentile needs to get through to God – that is the secret. Paul could not wait to tell the world. God had now sent Paul straight to the Gentiles, not to bring them into Israel but to bring them to Jesus. Paul did not need to take any of the Jewish tradition with him, just Jesus Christ. The Gentiles are now on absolutely equal terms with Jews. They are fellow heirs and will inherit everything promised. They are members of the same body and partakers of the same promise.

The word "partakers" means eating together. There is a difference between friendship and fellowship. Friendship is to sit down and just have a meal together. But at one chapel tea I remember eating a sandwich, taking a bite and putting it down and talking as I usually do, and when I picked it up again it was twice as small! I remember putting it down, picking it up again, taking another bite, and the next time I put my hand out, I put my hand on another hand. The minister sitting next to me was eating the same sandwich! That is partaking; that is fellowship. "Friendship" is to eat different sandwiches in each other's company; "partaking" is the word that means fellowship. To fellowship together, to partake together, means to share the same thing. In the Lord's Supper we eat of the same loaf. There is one loaf, one body. We partake of that loaf. We don't say that when we just have a normal tea together. We don't say, "We've partaken together." But when we come and share one loaf we say, "We've partaken of the Lord's Supper."

The Jews wouldn't even have a meal with Samaritans who were half-Jewish. It says in John's Gospel that when Jesus met the woman at the well and said, "Can I have a drink of water?" she was astonished because it says, "Jews do not use the same cup as the Samaritans" – meaning they did not partake from the same crockery. Here we have Paul saying Jews and Gentiles are now going to "eat" together at the same promise. All the promises in the Old Testament were made to the Jews, and you and I quote them and claim them without turning a hair. The Psalms were Jewish prayers and praises, and you and I use them in our devotions.

We have taken and eaten the same promises and we have taken it for granted, yet this was a secret that was kept for centuries and they never realised it. Paul says, "I've got the secret" – he told me, he revealed it to me direct. Here is the mystery of God, the mystery of Christ, the secret that can now be told – Gentiles and Jews are equal before God and can come through Jesus Christ, and Gentiles don't need to become Jews first.

Paul had had to fight for this principle all his life. Wherever he went and preached, some Jewish Christians would follow and talk about circumcision and say, "You ought to become Jews" – and everywhere Paul went, he fought that. He wrote his letter to the Galatians just to deal with this. He said, "Beware of the dogs, the circumcision group who would circumcise you." Paul was in prison because he was accused of bringing Gentiles to God—that is why he was in chains.

How does God share the secret? He shares it by word of mouth. That is how every other secret is shared. Somebody says to you, "Can you keep a secret?" and you're all ears. Have you ever said "No," to that question – "Don't tell me because I can't keep it"? Could you have sufficient self-discipline? Well, when you have a secret you want to share, and a secret that can be shared, a secret affecting everybody in the world, you can't keep quiet about it. Paul was chosen to tell this good news.

I recall a day when I had the privilege of going and telling a grief-stricken mother some news about a member of her family that was far better than she had dared to hope. I was bubbling over just to share this good news. I couldn't get to her quickly enough to tell her. To share good news is a lovely privilege. If you have good news for someone, it bursts out. You don't say, "I have a duty to go and tell someone this good news." It is a delight to do so, and this is what evangelism essentially should be. It should not be undertaken because we have a duty to go out and tell the world. We have had commissions on evangelism, books on evangelism. We have looked at the duty of it, but if you believe that the gospel is good news, then you want to go and tell people. It should bubble out.

Paul is bubbling over and he says, "God chose me to tell this." You see, if he had gone to the Gentiles before he had met Christ he would have gone in a spirit of patronage. Even if he had been told by God to go, he would have gone with a spirit of, "I am a Jew doing you a favour by sharing with you Gentiles what God has given to me. It is very good of me to come." Beware the patronage spirit, in which you think you are doing others a favour by taking them good news. When you have really got the good news you talk like this: "I am a debtor. I owe it to them to tell them. I am a debtor to both Jew and Greek. I've got to tell them. To me the privilege is given, the least of all the saints." That I should have the privilege of going and telling someone great news – that is evangelism; and it was how Paul felt. He could never get over this privilege. He called himself chief of sinners, least of the apostles, the lowest of all the saints. He just couldn't get over it – that God should use him to tell the secret to others.

What good news? He says, "I was made a minister...." May I say that there is one career that you can't choose for yourself. You can choose to be a butcher, baker, architect, indeed you can choose to be anything at all. There is one thing you can't choose to be and that is a minister of God's grace. Only God can make a minister. You can become an organiser, a cheerleader, a public orator, but you can't become a minister. It used to be said in English society that if a man had three sons, the eldest would inherit the father's business, the second would go into the army, and the third should go into the church. This was a kind of pattern that tended to happen, as if it was a matter of career.

I was shattered the other day when I saw a series of official publications on careers, and stuck right in the middle was a book on how to become a priest, as if it was simply a career, as if anybody could say, "I'd like to be a minister." Believe me, I am not a minister because I wanted to be. I didn't want to be; it wasn't my ambition, wasn't my intention. It's God who makes a minister. There are two things that make a minister: a gift of God's grace and a working of God's power. Paul says he was made a minister. Are you a young man whom God is wanting to make a minister? It would need a gift of God's grace and a working of God's power, because you haven't the gifts and you haven't the power to minister by yourself.

A minister to do what? To preach the unsearchable riches of Christ. One of the funniest experiences of my life was to appear before the Baptist Union Ministerial Recognition Committee. They wanted to put me on their accredited list and I said, "All right, well I'm willing to answer questions." So there we were. You know what one of the main questions was? There weren't many, but I'll never forget this one: "Do you realise that a Baptist pastor has to prepare two sermons a week, and do you think you could keep it up?" The questioner, who was himself a minister, clearly had some personal difficulty in spinning out his little store of knowledge week after week. Now, let's face it, if I were in the entertaining business, I would have had ulcers, because to use up material at the rate of an hour and a quarter, an hour and a half a week, is colossal. A television comedian told me: "Use a joke on television once and it's finished. You've got to find new material all the time. You've got to be packing it in. You've got to have scriptwriters piling this stuff into your brain so that you can just keep going. Even then you can only manage a series of maybe a dozen shows and then you're off, and you've got to recuperate." Paul says, "I was made a minister to preach the unsearchable riches of Christ," which means the inexhaustible wealth. I'm afraid you now know that if I were to preach for hours and hours, I would still have something to say. I could go on preaching for many decades and I would still have material. I would still have a problem of what to leave out, still have a problem of how to concentrate on certain things instead of packing so much in – "the unsearchable riches of Christ", what a privilege! You are never stuck for material. What a book! You can go through and through the Bible from cover to cover and still you find something new. Paul says, "To me, the least of all the saints, he made a minister to preach the unsearchable riches of Christ."

What is the object of it all? Why all this preaching? The answer is: to make all people see the plan that God has. That is what it is all about. Literally he says, "To turn the light on so that men can see." That is my job; I am a lamp lighter. Paul said, "...to light a lamp so that they can see the plan of God." God's plan is to unite all people in Christ. That is the mystery; that is the secret: Gentiles, Jews; black, white; rich, poor; clever, simple; east, west – it doesn't matter, I'm going to bring them all together in Christ.

How is he declaring that? The answer is: through the church. Those who talk of being Christians without the church are talking through their hats. You can't have Christianity without a church because that is God's visual aid; that is where you see his plan fulfilled: people who would normally never mix, together one in Christ. Fellow heirs, partakers of the same loaf, joint heirs, members of the same body – that is where people see the manifold wisdom of God being worked out. The word "manifold" here means "a variety of colours". That is rather interesting. It is God's will that people of every kindred and tribe and tongue should be in Christ. Where are people going to see that if there is no church? If each one of us can be a Christian all on our little own, where are people going to see the plan of God to bring people together like that? The church is as vital to Christianity as Christ is, for it is his Body, and a headless body is no use on earth – so "through the church".

This mystery of God was hidden in the Creator before all ages. Some people have told me that they think that God thought of turning to the Gentiles only after the Jews had turned Christ down, as if it was a kind of afterthought, a change of plan – that he offered the kingdom to the Jews, they said no, so he said, "All right, I'll give it to the Gentiles." According to Ephesians 3 he knew all along that he was going to do this. It was in his mind when he created the world. It was hidden in God who created all things. He knew all along what he was going to do, and he was going to go to the Jews first and then he was going to turn to the Gentiles.

Then, to complete the picture, he is going to bring the Jews back in at the end. Or as Paul puts it, in gardening language: Israel is cut off from its own roots since Christ came. You Gentiles have been grafted into the roots and you are growing on the Jewish stock now. You are using a Jewish Bible, you are worshipping the God of Abraham, Isaac and Jacob, but one day Israel is going to be grafted back in and we will all be one in Christ. God knew this; he doesn't change his mind as easily as that. He knew it all the way along. So he went to the Jews, he gave the Jews their own Messiah, who came and said, "I was not sent but unto the lost sheep of the house of Israel." He gave them the first chance, and when they turned it down, Paul in the name of Christ said, "Lo, I turn to the Gentiles" – and he did.

Hidden in the Creator, revealed through the church and, thirdly, observed by the angels. I want you to realise that angels watch us. It is the only way they learn the secrets of

God. Consider that for a moment. God says, "I'm making known my wisdom through the church to the principalities and powers in heavenly places." This has profound implications for us. Do you realise that when we worship and we say, "Therefore, with angels and archangels and with all the company of heaven, we laud and magnify your holy name", they are there watching?

When Paul discusses what kind of clothes you should wear in church he says, "Because of the angels." They notice what you put on – your Sunday best – they are watching. But the angels are looking down to see what God has in mind. When they see the church coming together, and the Gentiles and the Jews coming together, and people of all classes and cultures and colours coming together in Christ, the angels say, "So that's what God is on about. So that's what he wants. So that's his plan: making known to the principalities and powers through the church the manifold wisdom of God." You are called to be a witness not only on earth but to heaven; heaven watches us and that should produce in us a deep sense of responsibility.

"All this," says Paul, "gives us great confidence." God's plan in eternity has been realised in time in Jesus Christ. So now, with boldness and confidence we can come to God. That means that you may stop a man preaching, but you can't stop him praying. That means you may shut his mouth as far as men are concerned, but you can't as far as God is concerned. So he says: "Don't lose heart". I may be suffering, I may be in prison, but it is your glory. You should be thrilled that a Jewish Jew was ready to go to prison for you Gentiles, and you can't stop me praying. The two grand means that God uses to fulfil his purposes are preaching and prayer. If those two things are strong in a church, that church will be strong, for these are God's chosen agencies.

We turn to the next section. Paul says, "I bow my knees

for this reason...." He can no longer preach widely, he can no longer travel around telling everybody there is a great secret, but he can pray, and he does.

He prays for them because he wants them to carry on the preaching. This is a wonderful notion of one person telling another and then praying that the other will tell someone else, and so it is going to multiply. If only we just captured this simplicity of operations! It is so utterly simple. Do you know that if each believer in a town brought one person to Christ over the next twelve months, and those two did it again in the following twelve months, within five years there wouldn't be anybody living in that community who wasn't a Christian? It is so simple if we could just do that. Have you ever thought of praying for that? That you would lead one more person to Christ in twelve months? You work out the mathematics of it if you think I am wrong. England would soon be converted.

We discuss our methods and we find out this way of doing it, and that way of doing it, all of which is helpful, but the simple method of God is: preach and pray, share the secret. Pray that the person who has heard it will pass it on. So Paul says, "I pray for you now ... I bow the knee." A physical attitude helps a mental attitude. Standing in God's presence honours him. Lifting holy hands to him helps you spiritually. Kneeling helps you to pray. I think kneeling is a lovely attitude of prayer. "I bow the knee...." Here in a cell, chained to a soldier, Paul gets on his knees. What would the soldier think? Paul didn't care. If he had been able to get away privately, he would have done, because the Lord Jesus said, "When you pray, get into a room alone" – but Paul could not do that, so he decided to bow the knee and that was right.

Who did he pray to? He prayed to the Father. When you are praying, you are coming as a child. You are not coming as a citizen to a king, though you are coming to a King. You are coming as a child to a dad. "I bow my knee as to the Father." Now some people say, "You shouldn't think of God in human terms. God is wholly other, God is infinite, God is transcendent." They pile up the words. You will find in their prayers they keep putting the adjectives in front: transcendent, infinite God. Paul says, "I bow my knees to Father," and it is so much simpler. People say that this is anthropomorphism, which means to think of God just like a man. So when you talk about God's hand, God's feet, God's eyes, God's ears, God's mouth or God's arm you are guilty of anthropomorphism. Well, scrap the word and scrap the idea because the real truth is that man is made like God, and therefore, you can use these words.

A prayer at a prayer meeting made me smile. Some theologians and philosophers would have been horrified, but my heart was thrilled. Someone said, "Thank you for being so human." God is human, except that it really is the other way around. When we are most human we are being most godlike. So Paul says, "I pray to the Father". It is just like being in a family with him, and the reason is that every father on earth is made like him. It is not that we are making him like us, we are like him. A family on earth is a little reflection of what he wants to be. Every house on earth that has a father and a mother and children, and love, is a little picture of what God's plan for the ages is. So when you pray, say, "Father." It has been suggested you learn more about someone from his prayers than his preaching. Well, I want you to notice what Paul prays.

He prays five things for those people. When you pray for others, do you pray for these five things? Look at them. First of all, I want you to notice that he prays for their *inner man* rather than their outer man. Isn't it astonishing how often we pray for people's "outer man" and neglect to pray for their "inner man"? What do we mean by that? Well, my outer man you can see. It needs health, strength, food, clothes and shelter. Whenever you pray for those things, you are praying for the outer man. That is right, and Jesus told you to say, "Give us today our daily bread." But when you pray for others to whom you have spoken of the secret of God, do you pray for the inner man?

What is included in the inner man? A strong conscience, a strong will, a convinced mind, a loving heart. This is the more important because the outer man is going to finish one day; the inner man goes on. When you pray for someone, pray for their inner man, that they may be strong inside. They may not be strong on the outside, but to be strong inside is the more important thing. To be strong in heart, mind, and soul—that is where the strength is needed. Even physical weakness can be coped with as long as the inner man is strong.

The second prayer is to be *indwelt by Jesus*, taken over by his strong personality. Literally, it is that Jesus may be at home in your heart. I think that is a gorgeous phrase. What a translation! I pray that Jesus may be at home in your heart. You can't be at home if there are things in a house that you are uncomfortable about. If Jesus is to feel at home in our hearts, then our hearts must be the kind of home he feels at home in, and that involves quite a lot of self-examination.

Thirdly: that you may be *established*. The words used are "rooted" and "grounded". You watch a good gardener planting a rose tree: spreading out the roots carefully, then putting the peat, the soil and the fertilizer in, and treading it well in so that it is firm. Rooted and grounded, then you are going to get the beauty later. Paul prays that they may be rooted and grounded. You see, he knows that it is only too easy to be a Christian who is here today and gone tomorrow – "a burst of enthusiasm followed by chronic inertia" is a saying I recall. We can all start – we can all blaze away for a few weeks – but a person who is rooted and grounded will still be witnessing in forty years' time.

Fourth prayer: *that you may be enlarged*. One of the great dangers of becoming a Christian is that you become a small person, a little personality. I will tell you why: because many of the interests you have had, you have to drop, Christ tells you to, and you will need to develop new ones. Otherwise you become narrow in the wrong sense and your life shrinks. So Paul says, "I pray that you may explore the length, the breadth, the height, and the depth...." Live on a big map, be a big soul. We should not be called narrow, little people. People should be able to say, "What a big soul he is!" You have met people like this, haven't you? They have explored God so much that they have got big souls with a big heart and a big mind. I can think of some people like that. They may have had small bodies, but they have been big people. Oh, they have got such a big heart. They can cope with so many people. They have got such a big mind – they can learn new truths. A small mind has learned it all in the first year and never grows after that, but a big mind says, "I'm just paddling in the shallows of a mighty ocean. There's so much more to learn." That you may be enlarged and know the length, the breadth, the height, and the depth of the love which goes far beyond knowledge ... knowledge is good, but love surpasses it.

Finally, there is prayer that you may be *filled with God*. At the end of v. 19, "...filled with all the fullness of God." Talk about putting a quart into a pint pot! I will never forget when I went into a laboratory to see an exhibition of atomic energy. I discovered that in the tiniest atom, that you can't even see, there is a whole universe of little bodies moving around like the planets in the sky, and that God has somehow taken the whole universe and packed it into each atom. Paul is saying he can take a tiny little life such as yours, and he can take all his fullness and he can get it into your life. Don't ask me how. "To be filled with all the fullness of God" – if you are going to be filled with the fullness of God, then you have got to be emptied of everything else. It follows, doesn't it? So you are praying that you may be emptied of everything else so that God can fill you full to overflowing. That is how we should pray for other people – that they may be strengthened, indwelt, established, enlarged, filled.

Finally we come to 3:20–21 and I hardly dare to say anything about this. Do you know that in this little letter to the Ephesians, Paul uses every word in the New Testament for power except one, and that one is "violence". Might, strength, power are there. "Now to him, who by the power at work within us is able to do exceedingly, abundantly...." Paul is stretching his words to the limit now. "Exceeding, abundantly" – that's exaggeration isn't it? No! "...exceeding abundantly more than all we ask or think."

Why then do we not see more of God's work? Why do we not see more of God's power? We don't ask, and we don't think – that's all. He is able to do it. The God who flung the stars into space can do anything. Why don't we see more miracles? Well, we don't ask. When we ask, we can't imagine it happening. Never pray outside your faith, ask only for those things you can imagine happening – that you can expect to happen. Then you will find that he who is able to do exceeding abundantly above all that we ask or think will stretch your faith to ask for something bigger and bigger.

I read of a church that had not seen any growth for many years. They met together to ask what they should do about it, and they decided to ask specifically for a 10% increase in membership by the end of the year and they prayed for that. By the last day of the year they had 10% more members. Do you know their reaction? "Why didn't we ask for 20%?" A 10% increase was as far as their faith could go, so they asked for what they could think could happen and God did it. Don't pray for things that you can't believe will happen. Don't ever say, "Lord, convert all the people in my community" if you can't imagine it happening. God is able to do more, but he has chosen to work through our asking and thinking. That is why some of our prayers are not answered. We have asked maybe, but we didn't think it would happen.

"Now unto him who by the power at work within us is able to do exceeding abundantly above all that we ask or think...." What a promise to take! Isn't it great to feel that it's always going to be better, and that God is going to do more and more as we ask and think in the name of Jesus?

"Now to him be glory...." When he does what we have asked, we must be very careful to give him the glory. It is not our doing, it is the Lord's doing. It is marvellous in our eyes, but it is his doing. We must give him the glory in the church in Christ Jesus through the ages. Nobody must ever get the glory. If you hear any glory given to ministers, leaders, or members of a church, then tell them straight away, "You have given the glory to the wrong person because they are not responsible." It is not the church. The glory is *in* the church *to* God.

THE CHRISTIAN'S WALK
– in church

Read Ephesians 4:1–16

His authority and his appeal (1)

A. UNITY WITH DIVERSITY (2–12)
 1. Unity (2–6)
  a. The PRACTICE (human and visible) vv. 2–3
        Humility
        Meekness – patience – forbearance...the ingredients of peace
  b. The PRINCIPLE (Divine and indivisible) vv. 4–6
        The Spirit – one body, one hope
        The Lord – one faith, one baptism
        The Father – above, through, in all
 2. Diversity (7–11)
  a. The GIVER Ascended and descended
  b. The GIFTS What?
                Apostles – whole church
                Prophets – any church
                Evangelists – no church
                Pastor/teachers – one church
            Why?
                Equipment
                Service
                Building

B. MATURITY WITH CHARITY (13–16)
 1. Maturity (13–15a)
  a. The GOAL (13) – complete development
  b. The GROUND (14–15a) – constant doctrine
 2. Charity (15b–16)
  a. The BRAIN (15)
  b. The BODY (16)

A congregation I led moved into a new building and the first big question I then posed for them was this: "What kind of a church are we going to put into this building? Let us not think we have built a church, we have built a house for the church, that's all."

Paul the apostle is also concerned about this, and there are two vital characteristics he has outlined here in chapter four. Number one: a church that is characterised by *unity with diversity*. Number two: a church that is characterised by *maturity with charity*. If those words are a bit big, we will break them up small enough to digest as we go along. Bear in mind that Paul has the authority to talk about these things. Any man who has suffered for Christ can speak with authority. Any man who is in prison for building churches is a man to whom we must listen, and he says, "I, a prisoner of the Lord, chained...." He was there because he built churches, and he wanted to tell his readers what kind of a church to build.

Notice the appeal he makes. He asks us to walk worthy of the vocation with which we are called. To many people today the word "vocation" is connected with their job or career. "What is your vocation?" "Oh, well, I'm a teacher", "I'm a nurse", "I'm an architect," or whatever. However, the word "vocation" in the Bible is not concerned with your career but with your character – not with *what* you do, but *how* you do it. It really doesn't matter what job you have, your vocation is about whether you are doing that job to the glory of God and doing it well.

Vocation is the calling to which you have been called. Though, for example, I am a minister, a preacher of the gospel, my vocation is to be a good and a godly man. That is your vocation or, if you're a lady then your vocation is to be a good and godly lady. Paul says, "I, a prisoner, plead with you to walk worthy of your vocation." As I understand it, the word "walk" means to go in the right direction taking one step at a time. Nothing could be simpler, for that is the Christian life. It is taking one step at a time in the right direction.

Now let us look at the two characteristics of the church as Paul longs to see it. First of all: unity. These verses are super-charged in these ecumenical days. They have been discussed and debated, and the great debate has been this: some say on the one hand that the unity is broken and lost, and Christ's body is fragmented and we must all get together and put it together again like Humpty Dumpty – that we have lost the unity that Christ prayed for and that we have got to rediscover it and work for it and pray for it. On the other hand is a group who say the unity of Christ has never been lost. To quote the Keswick Convention text, "We are all one in Christ Jesus." The unity is there already – there is no need to work for it or pray for it, it's there. Which of these two groups is right? Both! I am not usually a diplomat, trying to please everybody, but I believe the *practise* of unity may be lost. I believe the *principle* of unity cannot be lost.

Just before the start of the first service in our new church building, a gentleman came in, knelt down on the floor and said a prayer. He was the vicar of the parish, a Mr Goddard. He slipped a little letter into my hand. He had written, "My Dear Pastor Pawson, I want to send you greetings in our Lord Christ to you all in your new home from both my people and myself. God be with you, bless you, joy you, and grace you. Peace be with you all. Yours in Christ." He worshipped in a very different way, but the unity was there. We can lose the practice, but we can't lose the principle.

Let me talk about both these. First of all, *the practise of unity*. Paul is primarily concerned with the unity within a local fellowship. He is writing to Ephesus. That is the most important point – where unity begins. Charity and unity begin at home for the Christian, which is within his own fellowship. I would hate to see a local fellowship divided over the ecumenical movement—that would be a tragedy. It would lose unity at the very point where it is needed most: a fellowship together.

Now what are the ingredients for practising unity in the fellowship? There are four: humility, meekness, patience and forbearance. If you lose those, you lose unity. Let us take them one by one. First: *humility*. What is the heart of humility? Is it being like Uriah Heep rubbing his hands and saying, "Ever so humble, ever so humble"? No. Humility is this: to see yourself as God sees you. If you only see yourself as others see you or, worse still, if you only see yourself as you see yourself, then you will not develop humility. But when you see yourself as God sees you, you can be nothing else but humble. Humility is necessary to keep unity. Proud people break it. Arrogant people break it. Humble people bring it.

The second thing is *meekness*. That means a person, not who is mild, not who is weak, but a person who is not concerned about their own reputation, their own rights or their own revenge, a person you can do anything to and they stay the same—they do not take offence. How easily fellowship is divided when people get offended over something. They were overlooked, or something was said that should not have been said. They are offended, and there is a little break or crack in the unity of the fellowship. You need meekness, because a meek person can never be offended.

Thirdly, you need *patience*. The literal Greek word means, "long-tempered", a word that has disappeared from the English language, though the expression "short-tempered" is still used. But we need to be long-tempered if we are going to maintain unity in the bond of peace.

The fourth thing is *forbearance*. Kenneth Taylor translates this so beautifully that no other word is needed but his phrase: "Making allowance for each other's faults."

Now given those four ingredients you can have the peace which is the cement that holds the church together – the bond of peace, of harmony. If a bunch of people with mixed temperaments, backgrounds, everything else, are going to have unity these are the four things we have got to have. If any one of these goes, we are going to see cracks appearing in the fellowship. That is the unity that you can lose, and it is the unity we are to practise.

Now the foundation of that unity we never lose. How do you build up this kind of peace? How do you get this kind of harmony? By remembering that, in fact, there is only one Spirit, one Lord Jesus Christ, and one God and Father of us all. Our unity is rooted and grounded in the kind of unity God has: three persons in perfect harmony. You never heard of the Father and the Son disagreeing. You have never heard of the Son and the Spirit falling out with one another. Jesus says, "I pray that they may be one as we are...." All unity is rooted and grounded in God's unity; the unity springs from the Trinity.

So Paul goes through the persons of the godhead. Firstly, if you feel a quickening of life in your church meeting, if you feel the Spirit of God touching you, do you realise it is the same Spirit touching the person sitting next to you? The same Spirit blows right along your pew and the same Spirit is moving in everybody's heart – one Spirit, and because there is only one Spirit, there is only one body. You can't have one breath and have more than one body. One Spirit; one body, and one hope of your calling. I can put it like this: we are all going to live together in heaven, then let us live together on earth. We only have one future before us, and that is the glorious future in Christ. We are all going to be living in one house, the Father's house, and since we have one Spirit who has given us this one body, and this one hope, that is a unity we can never lose. You can never say to another Christian, "I'm going to live in a different part of heaven from you." I know all the jokes about some Christians behind high walls in heaven, but that is just not true. There is no Bible foundation for it.

Secondly: *one Lord*. When you became a Christian, you came to the same person I did. You came in a different way, you came at a different time and you came with a different need, but you came to the same person. I met Jesus in 1947. When did you meet him? It was the same Jesus. "One Lord" – hence one faith; one baptism. You believe in that person so you can only be baptised into that person. We believe in Christ; we are baptised into Christ. Notice the order, incidentally. One Lord is standing there and we come to him with one faith, one baptism.

Thirdly, and this too is foundational, is that God is only one God and Father of us all. If it is only one Father, one dad, there is only one family. Every Christian you meet is your brother and sister. You can do nothing about that. This illustrates perfectly the unity we can lose and the unity we can keep. I think of when our children were small. They could lose their unity. We didn't always have the bond of peace maintained in our household. But however much they might have fought or argued, they remained brother or sister. Children – brothers and sisters – cannot do anything about that. They live in the same house whether they like it or not. They might have to have separate bedrooms for a time, but my children have only one father. They can't change him. They can't deny that relationship, and that is the balance in scripture. There is one Spirit, one Lord, one

God and Father of us all. That is the unity you cannot lose,
but you can maintain that unity by practising it in the bond
of peace as you are humble, meek, patient, and prepared to
make allowance for each other's faults.

Paul takes off at this point: "One God and Father of us all,
who is in all, and through all, and over all" – he can't stretch
that word "all" any more. He is describing the omnipotence
of God, his power over all. The omniscience of God is
knowledge of all; he is in it all. The omnipresence of God –
he is there everywhere. Paul is simply getting a big view of
God. "O magnify the Lord with me." Now all that is unity.

We move quickly on to diversity. I want to say to those
who are so anxious to get us all into one organisation and
under one department that God's unity is not uniformity.
Look at a tree. A tree is a unity; God made it a unity, yet
there are no two leaves alike. There is life – the same sap
is going into the whole thing and yet it is producing the
most remarkable variety. No two trees are the same; no two
people are the same. God can perfectly combine unity and
diversity. There is to be a diversity in the fellowship of the
church – a variety – and the variety will be in the gifts that
are exercised.

So Paul moves on. You have got the unity, but expect a
diversity, a variety of gifts. God does not give all the gifts to
one person. Nor does he give the same gift to each person.
Our ideas of the ministry are going to have to change at
this point. First, there is no division in the New Testament
between clergy and laity – there is only ministry, and
diversity of gifts. So let there be no division of clergy and
laity now – it is not divine; it is not his pattern.

Secondly, in church leadership there should not be the
thought: I am *the* minister of this church. I prefer the word
"pastor" because members are the ministers too. There is
a shared ministry. A teacher has been given a gift that puts

him in one position; others have been given gifts that put them in other positions. For when Christ got back to heaven he just poured out gifts on people. That was the only way he could continue working on earth. For the gifts were in Jesus – he is the one exception to what I have just affirmed. In Jesus Christ I see all the gifts. Don't you? For in him dwelt all the fullness of the godhead bodily. He had all the gifts. What was going to happen when he went back to heaven and took all his gifts with him? Well, he was going to pour them out on a lot of people, so that many – together – could continue what he could do alone, and that is his will for us now. Having ascended on high, he gave gifts to people so that we could go on doing his work – but do it together. He did not give all his gifts to one man so that one man could go on doing his work, that is not his plan.

Now there is a picture in Paul's mind as he writes here. I have stood in the Roman forum and looked at the magnificent road that leads down between the palace of Caligula and the senate house. It is a marvellous place to be. The centuries slough off and you stand there, and you can see the Roman armies marching down in triumph from the arch of Titus at the top of the way. They have been away and fought a war and they have come back victorious. Do you know what the general would have done when he came back? He would have divided the booty and given gifts to men. That is what Jesus did when he marched back to heaven triumphant. He divided the booty; he had got the gifts and he gave them out to people. He showered them upon us and he is sharing them with you and with me to build up his church.

These gifts vary tremendously – some of them apostles, some prophets, some evangelists, some pastors, some teachers. I thank God he spread them out. A church needs to have some people with the gift of evangelist. You need people with the gift of prophet, and that is a gift which is returning, for which I give thanks to God. All these gifts are to accomplish something. Look at your Bible now and you will probably see three words that we use in the wrong way: *equipment*, *services*, *building*. What do you think of when you hear those three words? Do you think of chairs and tables, overhead projectors, screens and maybe an organ? When I say "services", what do you think of? 10:45 a.m. or 6:30 p.m.? When I say "building" what do you think of? Do you know that when Paul uses those three words he isn't thinking of any of those things? Equipment of the saints — that means the personal resources you need to lead another to Christ. "Services" doesn't mean services of worship, it means the things you do for other people during the week. "Building" doesn't mean concrete, bricks, stone, it means people – for the equipment of the saints, for the work of the ministry, for the building of the church.

Spurgeon had a man come to him one day and say that he would like to do some work for the church. He asked the enquirer, "What is your daily job?" He said that he was a train driver. Spurgeon asked whether his assistant was a Christian. No? Then go and win him for Christ – that's your job for the church! Really Spurgeon was saying: come to church to get the equipment to go out into the world and serve, and build up the church of Christ in quantity and quality. That is really your task and mine.

Why does God give pastors and teachers? They are to support the church. It isn't the church that supports the pastor, it is the other way round. A lady said to me, "I come to the church to get my batteries recharged for another week." I thought that was great, and I thank God that she goes away with them recharged. That is what my job is. Why does God give prophets, evangelists, pastors and teachers, and spread the gifts out? He does it so that you can be built up and go out to serve, and that the church might be bigger and better, for it needs building up in both quantity and quality – a bigger and a better church because you have been equipped for the work of the ministry.

We move now to another great feature of the church which Paul wants to see: *maturity with charity*. God doesn't want a family of babies. I know some parents who love little babies and would like to keep them that size. Snuggle them, wash them, and look after them, and they are lovely. But you don't want to see a baby that doesn't grow up, do you? I have often discussed with parents what they think is the ideal age of children. Well I know the age at which you have least problems. Aren't children of three or four lovely? But you can't keep them that way. A girl of ten, or a boy of twelve – that's a nice age. You would like to keep them just at a stage; you have such a relationship with them. Until children go to school, mummy and daddy are infallible. Then teachers are infallible. Then they reach their teens and they are infallible – and you get this changing relationship.

I have never yet come across any parents who wanted to keep teenagers forever. I think they then hope they will grow up and mature pretty quickly. Babies are nice; children are nice, but the greatest satisfaction a parent can have is in seeing their child grow up to be a mature adult; a responsible person. How thrilling – what a joy it is to see your children maturing, making their own decisions rightly; growing up. You think, "Oh, what a privilege to be a parent."

God wants you to grow up. He wants a mature church, not babies – not childish Christians. How do you know when you have grown up? We used to have a strip of paper on the back of one of our bedroom doors, with inches on it and various little pictures. The children used to stand against it. How do you know when you have grown up? I'll tell you. You can measure it exactly. You have grown up when you have reached the stature of Jesus Christ, when you have got to be as big as he is. Not physically, but spiritually – that is the test. Your reaction to that may be, "Well, I'll never make it." Yes you will. Do you think God begins a job and leaves it half done? He who began a good work in you can continue it until it is complete. One day you will reach that. Press on towards it.

"To build up the church until we all attain to the unity of the faith and reach the stature of Jesus Christ." Do you know what Christ's purpose was in coming to earth? Somebody has put it like this, and it is an unusual way to put it: it was to produce a race of Christs. Just let that sink in. Christ came to produce a race of Christs—a whole lot of himself; multiply himself over and over again until you have got a church full of Christs. It almost seems blasphemous to say it. Yet, that is what Paul is talking about: "Until we all get to be like him; until we've all grown up to the stature of Jesus Christ."

How do you tell when a person is childish? I'll tell you: when they keep changing their mind about what they believe. They read a new book and suddenly they have changed all their ideas about Christianity. They go and hear another speaker and suddenly it has all switched again. You really can't keep track of them; they are keeping up with the latest fashionable ideas all the time. Paul says, "I don't want you to be children tossed to and fro with every little wind of doctrine, blown here and there by men who can manipulate the Word of God." The word he uses was used in ancient days for those who manipulated dice. We would say: for those who can manipulate cards with sleight of hand. There are some people who can juggle texts as easily as a gambler can juggle a pack of cards, and a childish person will be misled. We will just hear a text here and a text there and think it is all right. A grown-up person isn't shaken. A mature Christian says, "I know what the faith is. You can't fool me with this sleight of hand. I believe the gospel, the truth once delivered to the saints. You won't shift me around." You have got a mature person who knows what he believes and stays right there. You see that maturity comes from truth. The goal of maturity is Christ, but the ground of maturity is the truth about Christ. When we know the truth about Christ we have got the foundation on which we can grow and build a life that becomes more and more like him, until finally we all believe the same thing.

I am often asked inside and outside churches what I think of the ecumenical movement and the scandal of divisions among people. I would love to scrap every denomination or label if I could. I am trying to work and pray towards that. But having stated that, I will tell you what I believe. I believe the greatest scandal of the church today is not that we have different labels, and not that we call ourselves "Anglican", "Methodist", "Baptist" or what have you, it is that we do not believe the same things. It is that you can move from one church to another and hear a different version of Christianity.

Now people are not even sure if we in the church believe in the deity of Christ or not, or even whether there is a God who is alive or not. That is the scandal, and that scandal will disappear as we all grow up into the unity of the faith and are no longer tossed to and fro by the latest theologians, the latest ideas and books, and believe and speak the same things about Jesus. One day, pray God, you will be able to say to anybody you meet, "You go to any church you like and you'll hear the truth about Jesus, and you'll find him," that's the day for which I long—the unity of the faith.

Having said that, I must add one last word: it's not just the unity of the faith, of the truth. There is "speaking the truth in love". I understand the little girl who prayed like this one day: "Lord, make all the nice people good and all the good people nice." Do you understand that prayer? Let me put it in this context, "Lord, make all the sound people loving, and all the loving people sound." It is possible to have such a zeal for the truth that you don't have love for people. Alas, it is also possible to have a loving, nice, kind person who doesn't seem to have grasped the truth. It is maturity, integrity – living, speaking, dealing truly in love – that is going to bring about the real maturity.

Truth without love becomes too hard; love without truth is too soft. Put them together and you have got exactly what you have in Christ. Christ was a man of truth. He always spoke the truth even though it hurt. He spoke the truth about God, the truth about men, the truth about the future. He always spoke the truth, but he spoke it in love. Even when he took a whip and lashed people out of the temple he did it in love, for love of those for whom that was meant to be a house of prayer. Speak the truth in love.

Paul now uses a biological metaphor. He talks again about a body and a brain. Somebody has said that his grammar is almost as difficult to dissect as his physiology! He does get very involved with some of his pictures, but now he gets involved in a body with its joints, ligaments and organs. Yet it is a picture of a body that is operating in love, every single part of it fitly framed together. Your joints are among the most important parts of your body. Some discover that if a bit of rheumatism comes, joints are very important. The separate pieces of your body are not much use unless they are fitly jointed together and can operate in a co-ordinated way. You may have many gifts, but without love the joint is missing. Indeed, one of the things that sometimes happens to joints later in life is that the liquid that lubricates them goes. The liquid that lubricates the members of the church is love. Then the body is fitly framed together, every joint applying just what is needed.

The body must not only be jointed together, each thing to each other, it must all be joined properly to the brain so that the brain can control it. So Paul writes of, "... the whole body fitly framed together growing up into him who is the head." Contact with each other, contact with him and you have the perfect relationship – that is the church I want to see. That is the church I love to help to build, a church that is a body of members joined together and responding perfectly to the head. Then we have a church that we can praise God for.

I finish with this matter of love. Child psychologists have told us that in a family it is more important for father and mother to love each other than for either to love their children. I wonder if you understand that? I will tell you why this is: it gives security. A child who sees father and mother arguing all the time will feel alone, insecure and frightened. That will grow up with him or her; staying with them throughout life. In the same way, I want to say this: it is more important for the world outside that Christians in a local church love each other than it is for us to love them. Don't misunderstand me and quote me out of context. You can go out and try and win people for Christ until you are blue in the face, but if you introduce them to a church where Christians don't love each other, your work will be undone; you will have an awful difficulty. But if outsiders can come in and say, "Look how these Christians love each other," you are halfway there. You have opened up their personality; you have shown them that God is love – in your relationships with each other.

We finish this study with a story of an Indian Christian who came to Edinburgh in 1910 to speak to the World Missionary Conference held in that city, an epoch-making conference. The Indian spoke on behalf of all the people in India who had benefited from those who had gone from this country to preach the gospel there. He said this to all those missionary societies gathered there: "You have given us so much. You gave us men and women; you gave us money; you gave us literature; you gave us hospitals, nurses, and doctors. You have given us so much, and for this we thank God. But I ask you to give us one thing more: give us friends." He was asking for love. He was asking for people who would go, not to patronise but to get alongside. That is why Paul writes of the whole body building up itself in love into him who is the head. It will do what God intended it to do.

THE CHRISTIAN'S WALK
– in society

Read Ephesians 4:17–5:20

A. CONDITION (4:17–24)
 1. Pagan (17–19)
        Ignorant; Insensible; Indecent; Insatiable
 2. Christian (20–24)
        Revelation; Repentance; Renovation
        Regeneration; Reformation

B. CONDUCT (4:25–5:4)
 1. Relationships – hurtful or helpful?
        False or frank (4:25)
        Gossiping or gracious? (4:31–32)
 2. Emotions – callous or caring?
        Resentful or righteous (4:26)
        Tempered or tender (4:31-32)
 3. Ambitions – getting or giving?
        Stealing or sharing? (4:28)
        Greed or gratitude (5:3–4)
 4. Words – corrupt or constructive? (4:29)
        Coarse or clean (5.4)
        Silly or serious (5.4)
 5. Characters – lustful or loving?
        Sensuous or sacrificial? (5:2–3)
        Filthy or fragrant (5:2–3)

Appeals – Don't gratify the devil (4:27) Don't grieve the Spirit (4:30)

C. CONSEQUENCE (5:5–14)
 1. Life or death (5–7) 2. Light or darkness (8–14)

D. CONSIDERATION (5:15–20)
 1. Simple – Intoxication; sorrows (15–18a)
 2. Sensible – Inspiration – songs (18b–20)

4:17–end

Would you say that Christianity is a way *of* life or a way *to* life? Long before the word "Christianity" was thought of, our religion was called "The Way". It was a title Jesus gave himself but it became the title of the religion he founded. When the Pharisee Saul went to Damascus to arrest people whom we would call Christians, he was given authority to arrest any of "The Way" and put them in prison.

Is Christianity a way to life or a way of life? My answer is: both. If you neglect either, you have not got the full understanding of the Christian religion. It is both – in a particular order. You come to Christ and you find the way to life, and then you work that out in a way of life. You don't try to live the Christian way of life first and hope that that will lead you to life. You find life first and then you live it. So Christianity is a way to life *and* a way of life.

In the first three chapters of Paul's letter to the Ephesians, he is dealing with Christianity as a way *to* life. It is inspiring, thrilling and exciting. In the second half of this little letter he is dealing with the way *of* life—not so exciting, not so inspiring but much more instructive. Not so exciting and yet much more real because this is where it all has to be lived. It is no use living with your head up in the clouds of heaven unless your feet are on earth. It is here that you have got to live out the Christian life.

Paul begins this passage most emphatically, "I affirm and testify" – and those are two very strong legal words. He is swearing; he is using the strongest words a Christian could use. He is saying one thing: you can never walk two ways; you cannot have both. I will put it like this in a cliché that you may remember: you can't tack the cross onto your old life. You must nail your old life to the cross. You cannot

111

possibly say, "I want to add Christianity to my life as it is. I want to add it to all of the rest I have got." It is either/or, and Paul is saying: I affirm and testify you've got to leave behind your old way of life if you're going to enjoy the new way. You can't walk two ways.

One of the reasons why some Christians don't enjoy God as they should, and don't find the Christian life as wonderful as it can be, is precisely because they are trying to walk two ways, and you can't. It is a difference between seeing some people go to the swimming pool and dive straight in and come up gasping with the shock of the cold water and saying, "It's wonderful, come on in," and somebody miserably climbing down the steps a toe at a time and they stand there just shivering and wondering whether to go further. Of course they look miserable. Until you decide to leave the past behind and plunge right into Christianity, you can't enjoy the new life. So Paul is going to talk about the new life in this passage and he talks first about the principle of the new life – what it is all about – and then he is going to work it out from v. 25 in practice: therefore this is how you do it.

Let us look first at the new life in principle. He says that you can't have both. I remember as a boy sometimes my mother would call a group of us from the garden and she would say when we arrived at the back door, "Wash all that mud off your hands because I've got some cakes for you." We jolly well had to go and get rid of the mud before we could have a handful of cake, and we were glad to. Paul is saying precisely the same thing here. God says to you: get rid of the mud, I have got new life for you; leave your former way of life behind you, I have got something new for you and you can't have it until you've got rid of that – you have got to leave the one behind if you are going to enjoy the other.

The first word under the principle of new life is *tradition*. He is saying: I want you to leave behind the way that everybody else lives—the traditions in which you were brought up; the way of life that your neighbours lived. You must leave behind the tradition of living all around you. In very strong language he then describes the condition of people who don't know Jesus Christ. There are two things that characterise their traditional way of life: one is an ignorant mind; and, two, a hardened or calloused heart. Now how did they get this way and how does it show? Take first an ignorant mind. That doesn't mean that an unbeliever can't be clever. He can have a string of degrees after his name, he can have all the "A" levels he's tried for, he can have studied for a lifetime and read books. He can be brilliant and clever and yet he can be ignorant. Sometimes I almost feel sorry for some people I meet who in their own field are brilliant – they have knowledge that I can't even reach. They could perplex me with the science of their career, yet ask them about God and they are not even up to the primary standard in the Sunday school. Just sheer ignorance about God, and yet they are clever and they know so much; they have got a brilliant career. They could do almost anything they turn their hand to, yet ask them about the things that matter most and they are not even children, they are just ignorant. Paul says their mind is characterised by three things. First it is *futile*. Now that is a very interesting word. It means to go around in circles. It means that life is like a roundabout—you get on, you have a great time while you are on it, and you go round and round and you get off just where you got on and you have got nowhere. These brilliant men with all their achievements, all their intellect, go round and round, and at the end of life they get off just where they got on. They haven't got anywhere. It is a futile mind that can't see where life is going and what it is all about.

The second thing he says is that they have a *darkened* mind. It is as if they can't see. A man jokingly said to me,

"You'll never get me to see the light." He was saying, "I've got a dark mind. I live in the shadows, I can't see," and he was walking around as if he was blindfolded.

A third word he uses here is *alienated*, which means that not only are people who don't know Christ ignorant, but that they were not always like that. At some point they have turned down the knowledge of God. At some point God has spoken to them. Maybe it was through a grandmother telling them about Jesus; maybe through a sunset; maybe through the sound of a hymn coming out of a church door; maybe just through creation or through their conscience – but at some point God has spoken to them. An alienated mind is a mind that was once open but is now closed, a mind that has said no to God at some point. The word "alienated" means there was once a link that has now been broken. The mind of the unbeliever is not a mind that is dark because it never had any light, it is dark because it once had some light and turned away towards the shadows. Now that is an ignorant mind. What is that due to? Paul says that behind the ignorant mind is a hardened heart.

Have you ever been to Napsbury in Yorkshire? There is a very deep ravine and the river flows through the bottom. If you walk along the riverside you come to a cave and you will find a piece of string hanging up in the cave and, attached to the piece of string, a bowler hat, an umbrella, a handbag, all sorts of things. If you look at them closely, they are all turning to stone. There is water dripping onto them from the roof and the water has so much mineral that it is depositing it on any object you hang up. Provided you are patient enough to go back after ten years you can have a stone bowler hat. I think a stone cap would be a wonderful thing for golfing – it would keep your head down! You can hang up anything and you can turn it into stone. The word Paul uses here of the heart of the Gentiles is exactly that word:

it is the word "petrified" or "calcified". It is a word used of joints that go solid because they have calcified. Paul says that the ignorant mind is due to a hardened heart. It refers to someone who has deliberately toughened himself, who has closed his heart, who has hardened it against the tender call of God. There was a point when he was tender and soft and when God could touch him tenderly, and he said, "No I'm not soft, I'm tough," and he hardened his heart. Paul says that you hardened your heart by stimulating your feelings too much. The sensual becomes insensitive. It is a remarkable thought that the more you are concerned with stimulating your own feelings, the less you will be sensitive to the feelings of others. That is an insight that the Bible gives us, which is very remarkable. There we have your former way of life—that is the kind of thing you were heading for—an ignorant mind and a hard heart.

When you try to talk to some people about the Lord Jesus Christ, you just see those two things: even if you can persuade their minds of the truth of what you say, their hard hearts will still not respond. What dark minds and hard hearts people can get who have alienated themselves from God. Now, Paul is saying, the first principle of new life is that that tradition has gone. You leave it behind; you never touch it again. If you go back to an ignorant mind and a hard heart, you cannot enjoy new life.

The second principle of new life is *transposition*. An organist will know what that means. To change the key and to transpose a hymn tune is to lift it to a higher or a lower key. In Christ your life has been lifted to a higher key. You didn't learn from Christ to have an ignorant mind or a hard heart. That is not how you learned to live the Christian life. You learned the opposite in him, and that came about in two stages: you heard about Christ and you were taught in him.

Notice both: the first step in getting new life is to hear

about Christ. Christianity hits you through the ear. Somebody spoke to you about Jesus. You were a long way away from him and you heard about him – but the second stage was that having come to Christ and come into Christ you are now being taught in him. You still need teaching. You needed teaching before you found Christ and you need teaching afterwards. You heard about him, now you are taught in him but everything you have been taught in Christ says: leave the old life behind, don't try and bring it with you – leave all your luggage behind. Just come yourself and he will replace your old luggage with new possessions in him that are absolutely wonderful.

The third principle of new life is the principle of *transformation*, which is the principle of changing your clothes. According to Paul, a Christian is now in a position to change his clothes. Some go to worship in what used to be called "Sunday best" – special Sunday clothes. I hope that you regularly put off your dirty clothes and put on clean clothes. Paul is saying here that a Christian is now in a position to open the new luggage that God has given him, and inside he finds new things to put on. But you can't put on clean clothes unless you take the dirty ones off. You don't wear two hats at once. I did once see a lady with two hats on and she had put one little one on the back of her head and forgot that she had put one on, and put another one on, but it was silly. You can't wear two sets of clothes in the Christian life. You can't wear your old clothes and your new ones. Paul says that a Christian has learned to leave the old way of life behind. He has learned in Christ that his life is to be lived in a higher key, and he has learned in Christ that he can actually take certain things off that are dirty and put certain things on that are clean. In other words, a Christian has a new wardrobe. He can change his nature. It is the devil's lie that you cannot change human nature. You can't change your old nature, no, but you can *put it off* now that you are in Christ. You can *put on* a new nature, and a Christian is in the happy position of being able to put off certain things that belong to his old nature and put on things that belong to his new. Now all this sounds a little vague, doesn't it? So let us come down to the specific. What kind of things do you put off in putting off the old nature? What kind of things do you put on in putting on the new nature? Let us be absolutely down to earth. What is he talking about? Three things in particular should characterise a Christian's new life: truthfulness, trustworthiness and tenderness. Now let us go through them. Take truthfulness – it is terribly important that we learn truthfulness, and it is not an easy thing to learn. It is interesting that you always have to teach your children to speak the truth. You never have to teach them how to lie, they will learn that naturally. It belongs to their old nature to be false. There are many ways to be false. One is to tell a deliberate lie, another is not to say anything. You can live falsehood. You cannot let people know what you really think about them or feel about them, and that is falsehood. The more sophisticated a society gets, the more false people get with each other, putting on a social veneer that hides real people.

So you can have a social contact with someone and you can have talked, you can have met them, you can have had a cup of tea together, and neither of you knows what the real person thinks. Neither of you knows what the other person is really like. Sometimes I am asked to provide a reference for someone. I am always glad when they have let me know first – that is just a little hint. When I look at the questions I am asked, sometimes I have to either say to the person or say to the one who has asked for the reference, "I'm sorry, I've only seen them on Sunday. I've seen them in church and we're all on our best behaviour in church. I honestly don't know what they are like on Monday morning. I honestly don't know what they are like with their colleagues." Of course they don't know what I'm like either.

Now falsehood belongs to the old nature. The old nature, the older it gets, the more it wants to cover up, the more it wants to hide, the more it plants a privet hedge and puts up lace curtains, and the more it wants to say, "Don't come too near me except when I'm ready to meet you. Oh dear, I wish you hadn't come now. If only I'd known you were coming I'd have tidied up the front room. Don't find me as I really am." Paul teaches us that, in practice, to live a life of truthfulness is to let people know who you really are. It involves truthfulness in conversation and truthfulness in emotion. Those are not easy. Let every one of you speak the truth with his neighbour. That can cause difficulties and it raises all sorts of questions.

My grandfather once used the phrase in a sermon "white lie". There was a shout from the gallery and someone called out, "Nay lad, they're all black 'uns." That was in a place where people really did let each other know what they were thinking. Sometimes you do have a problem here. I remember one young man who became a Christian and he came to me and said, "I thought we had to speak the truth to everybody when we became a Christian." I said, "Yes, Don, that's right. What's the matter?" "Well," he said, "It just gets you into trouble. Our next door neighbour has just redecorated a bathroom and she wanted us to go in and see it and tell us what we thought of it. I said, "It's terrible." He said, "Before I was Christian, I wouldn't have told her that. Now I am a Christian, we have got to speak truth with one another so I told her. She's not speaking to us now."

Well of course he was on the right lines but he had not read a little further. There is something in v. 29 to cope with that situation. To speak the truth with one another means being honest when you are asked a question. Do you mind if I do this? "Yes I do mind, but go ahead and do it – that's just me" is a more honest answer than "No, I don't mind" when you are going off and saying, "I don't want them to do that." Let everybody speak the truth with his neighbour. Why? Because you are members of one body, members of one another. If the members of a body don't convey accurate messages to each other, the body can't operate as a body. It is very important that the members of the body convey accurate messages to the other organs and members, or you can't co-operate. That is true of a physical body; it is true of the spiritual body. Now not only are we called to be honest in conversation but in emotion. We come to a strange verse, which says: be angry and do not sin. The devil loves people to bottle anger up, and so if you go to bed still angry you have given the devil an opportunity to work overnight. He will even work in your sleep. So never let the sun go down on your anger or you are giving the devil a wonderful opportunity to burn up your heart inside. I suppose it is true that the more sophisticated society becomes, the less people show their anger and the more they nurse it inside. The devil can use that to poison the atmosphere. It goes on burning until it festers. In your anger, *do not sin*—that is the qualification. We are not here given a blank cheque to lose our temper whenever we feel like it. It has got to be the right sort of anger – the anger that Jesus had. He was angry whenever children were hurt. He was angry whenever the poor were exploited. He was angry whenever somebody who couldn't defend himself was attacked. Most of the things that make us cross are the things that cross *our* will – the things that we wanted to do and can't. That sort of anger is not to be let out except to God to be cleansed. Never go to bed angry or the devil is right there in the bedroom and you will wake up in the morning with a spiritual hangover and you have given the devil an opportunity.

Here then is the first characteristic. It is a big one, a tough one. Put away falsehood – that belongs to the old nature. Put on integrity, truthfulness, honesty of speech and of feeling so that people know where they are with you and they know what you are saying and they know how you are feeling. Then the body can operate together and we are not hiding from each other.

The second is closely related to it – trustworthiness; to be able to be trusted. We have put our trust in Jesus; others ought to be able to put their trust in us. There are two sorts of trustworthiness mentioned here: those who can be trusted with other people's goods, and those who can be trusted with words. Let us take the first: goods. It should go without saying that a Christian cannot steal. He has finished with taking from other people what he has no right to have. But the interesting thing is that the motive for not stealing and for working honestly in a hard day's work is this: that he may switch his life right round and be able to give to others. Whenever a man steals, he is taking something from others, and Paul says a Christian has put that away and he has put on a life that is giving to others. Let a man that has stolen steal no more that he may have the opportunity to give to people what they have no right to have—that is the Christian life. Not to take from people what he has no right to have but to give to people what they have no right to have – and that is a much better way of life. Downright honesty is part of the Christian's new life.

What about honesty of words? To be trusted; to say the right thing at the right time in the right way – that is a real trustworthiness. Whoever does not say the wrong thing is a perfect man, according to James in his letter. So if you have never said the wrong thing, you are perfect – you have arrived. You are a saint through and through. You don't need to press on toward the mark, you have reached it if you have never said the wrong thing. Have you never said the wrong thing? Of course, we forget a lot of the things we have said. That is how we have managed to live with our conscience. But Paul says that a Christian is to live a life of trustworthiness, which means he can be trusted to say the right thing at the right time in the right way.

One of the habits that can come back to you from your old life is the habit of bad speech. The word Paul uses is "foul" speech. I have noticed that nearly every case of a Christian who has been accustomed in his former life to swearing a lot, as soon as he becomes a Christian he stops swearing. But also, some years later, he finds himself in a position where he swears again, when the temptation to revert to the old speech comes back. Paul is saying that you must not let that come back. The right thing at the right time in the right way. Look at the three phrases. The *right thing* – only such as is good for edifying; the right *time* – as fits the occasion; and the right *way* – that it may impart grace to those who hear. "Let your speech," says Paul in another place, "be always seasoned with salt," which means with grace.

We used to do this in our family: if somebody was just about to say the wrong thing, somebody else in the family said, "T-A-K-T" which spells nothing to anybody else but to us spells "tact". It was just a little family signal meaning: you are putting your foot in it. We would try to say that to each other, and it is really what this is about. Tact – saying the right thing at the right time in the right way. That is trustworthiness.

Otherwise people are afraid that whenever you open your mouth you will put your foot in it. They don't feel safe with you because they wonder what you will say next.

Now here is the final thing that Paul really comes down to – *tenderness*. I suppose that the blows of life can do one of two things to you. They can either make you tough or tender. Some people they make tough, but if you have got a very tough piece of steak, the best way is to take a hammer and just bash it, hit it until it is tenderised. Some people become very tough as life rains its blows upon them, but some people become tender. A Christian is to become tender. He will have blows, he will have hard knocks – no Christian has an easy life – but he is to develop tenderness. His old nature would develop toughness; his new nature will become increasingly tender. That tenderness is towards God on the one hand and people on the other. A tenderness toward God is this: it means knowing when you have hurt God, knowing when you have grieved the Holy Spirit, knowing when he is upset and unhappy. I suppose that it is easier to know when you can see a person whether you have upset them, and you can't see the Holy Spirit. It implies a great tenderness of spirit if you know when you have made the Holy Spirit of God unhappy.

Here is an amazing thought. I do not know of this thought in any other religion in the world: that God has feelings. It is said in one statement in the Book of Common Prayer I believe, that God is "without body, parts, or passions". That statement is two-thirds correct. He is without body and parts, but he is not a God without passions. He is a God with feelings, deep feelings, and you can hurt those feelings. You can cause the Holy Spirit sadness and sorrow. It is bad enough to know that you have caused sorrow to an earthly person, but to know that you have caused sorrow to a heavenly person—that is real tenderness.

We are to be so tender that we know when the Holy Spirit is unhappy about us. We know we have upset him. I can tell you why we upset him, why we make him sad: because he has sealed us for a day of redemption, which means he has stamped us for a day when we are going to be entirely free from these things that are wrong. Every time we go wrong now, he thinks, "Oh dear, that person has taken a step backwards. I thought they were coming on well, I was leading them on and now they have slipped." It is as if you are trying to teach someone how to do something and they do quite well, and then suddenly they make a hash of it and you are unhappy and you think, "Oh dear, we'll have to start again and take them on."

The Holy Spirit who sealed you for the day of redemption when you are set completely free from self and sin, is grieved when you slip back. Do you realise when he is upset? Do you know when he is unhappy? Do you realise that you have grieved him? That is tenderness. The other thing, of course, is that within the Christian family certain things can hurt each other. Don't ever go to a church expecting that you will not be hurt in that church – you will, because the members of it are not perfect. If you are thrown together, you will hurt each other and the closer you will come together the more likely you are to do so.

Here are the things that hurt in a fellowship: bitterness, wrath, anger, clamour—which means to shout at each other and raise your voice; slander or insult, and malice. These are the things that cause the hurt. So Paul says be tender-hearted not only to the Spirit of God but to each other, and forgive each other. Believe me, you won't be long in a church before you have something to forgive someone else. You won't be long in a church before someone else has something to forgive you for. If you don't forgive in a church, I ask you, where can you forgive? If you are not prepared to forgive those who belong to Christ, where will forgiveness ever start? Why should we forgive each other? I'll tell you – because God accepted you as you were. God in Christ forgave you. He didn't say, "Get rid of this, that, and the other, and then I'll forgive you." He said, "I'll take you as your are. I want

123

you in my church and I'll take you right as you are, and I'll forgive you for Christ's sake." Well, if he can accept you as you are, you can accept me as I am, I can accept you as you are, and we'll go on from there. Tender-hearted in forgiving one another as Christ forgave you.

You will never have to live the godly life without God. Isn't that thrilling? God doesn't sit up in heaven and say, "Now you try and live like me. You climb up the ladder all by yourself until one day you are like me." He says this: I have created in you a new nature which is perfectly made in righteousness and holiness and you can take off the old clothes of your old life and you can put on the new clothes.

One of the delights I think of being baptised is that after you have been washed clean, you come out and put on new clothes. Thereby hangs a symbol, and the symbol is that after Christ has washed you clean, you can now put on the new clothes of the new nature. It is as if he is holding out to you from his wardrobe a new nature for you to put on and he says: take off those dirty clothes; take off all your toughness and put on this tenderness; take off all your falsehood and your social veneer and put on this truthfulness; take off all your old untrustworthiness and put on this trust. Wear me and put me on.

5:1–20

It is a thrilling moment when a baby is born but there are certain milestones afterwards, which stand out as great moments also. One is when the baby begins to talk, but I think one of the most exciting is when a baby begins to walk those few faltering steps, with the parent wanting to hold the baby and yet holding back because you want them to walk. Their first few steps are taken. You remember that day when your baby began to walk. Now the same is true of spiritual babies—it is thrilling when a soul is born again and someone becomes a Christian and begins the new life, and it is even more thrilling when they start to walk. To walk means to take one step after another in the right direction. It is as simple as that. Walking is not very spectacular but it is so healthy. Most of us can walk further than we can run. If we walk, we are doing something that is good for us and that will get us somewhere.

Watchman Nee, the great Chinese Christian who was imprisoned for the Lord's sake, wrote a study of Paul's letter to the Ephesians entitled *Sit, Walk, Stand* and these are the three things that Paul tells you to do in this epistle. In chapter one he writes, "God has made us sit with Christ in the heavenly places." That is where you sit spiritually – your body may be here but your spirit sits in heaven. But your body is still on earth and your body can walk. So, having said that is where you sit, Paul now teaches that you must learn to walk. Then, at the end of Ephesians, in chapter 6, he says that when you are in the battle you must stand. So the Christian must learn three things: how to sit, how to walk, and how to stand.

The word "walk" occurs three times in this passage. It is there in 5:2, "walk in love". It is there in v. 8, "walk as children of the light." It is there in v. 15, "walk not as unwise men but as wise." There are three things to learn if you are going to walk the Christian life. Let me deal with two temptations. First, once you have become a Christian and sat down with Christ in heavenly places, the temptation is to go on sitting and do nothing more. You never get anywhere. You don't make progress. The other temptation with young Christians is to want to run before they can walk – to want to do something pretty spectacular for God, to want to do something great, something startling, yet God just wants you to learn to walk, just to move forward steadily in the right direction, and we would so love to run. Maybe you will one day, but learn to walk first or you will come a cropper if you try to run. Now the three things you need to learn if you are going to walk the Christian life are these: you need to learn the principle of *imitation*, secondly the principle of *illumination*, and thirdly, the principle of *intoxication*, and these three together lead to a good walk in the Lord.

The first is the principle of *imitation*. Most of the things we learn in life, we learn through imitating others. Most habits we pick up from other people. When you are young, there is a tremendous pressure on you to imitate others, to go with the crowd, to do what everybody else does, to conform. Now you don't want to conform to the elders when you are young but you want to conform to the young when you are young. So you imitate. Little children imitate their elders, teenagers imitate their contemporaries, but we are all imitating. Now that is not a bad thing, provided above all you are imitating the right person.

Every one of us is going to be a mimic in one way or another and the Greek word Paul uses here is "mimic". Therefore be mimics of God. Somebody said that Christians should be practising to be God, and there is something in this. Who are you going to imitate in life? Paul is saying: set your sights for your imitation on the very highest person you know – don't imitate other people but be imitators of God. The sad thing is that if you imitate other people you are imitating those whom Paul calls children (or sons) of disobedience. If you imitate other people, sooner or later you will find yourself disobeying God because other people do this. If you imitate them, you will disobey God also. There are some pretty horrible words used now, nasty words that have a horrible smell about them. The first three are concerned with immorality, impurity and covetousness. If you imitate others, sooner or later you will do these things, and so will I.

Immorality – the word means quite literally sex outside marriage, but the interesting thing about this word is that its root meaning is to sell. It means to treat people as things, to treat people as commodities who can be bought and sold. It is a very interesting word. The basic meaning of immorality is to treat people as things. Do you find it interesting that most of the slang words that young people use for members of the opposite sex treat people as less than people? If you study language, so often it turns out that we are treating each other as things and not as people to be loved.

The second word needs no definition, it means quite simply "dirt". The third word, "covetousness", again needs no definition. Philips translates it as, "grabbing anything you want, or the itch to get your hands on what belongs to other people." Now why does Paul link together immorality, impurity, and covetousness? The answer is very simple: all three of them are self-indulgence. All three of them are living to grab, to get, to be greedy for what I want. That is the thread that ties those three things together. Paul is saying that is what will happen if you imitate other people.

Then he goes on to a second group of three words: filthiness, silly talk, and levity. The reason he goes on to this is very simple. He knows that most of us begin not by doing these things but by talking about them. If you allow these things to creep into your words, it will not be long before they creep into your deeds. Now this is certainly true at school. Cast your mind back to your school days. Before you did anything wrong, you talked about it and you joked about it with the others at school – that is how it started.

So Paul says these three things, and Kenneth Taylor translates it like this: "Dirty stories, foul talk, and coarse jokes." Now you may have never done certain things but Paul is saying that even talking about them is the first step and leads to that. What effect do these things have on our lives?

Paul says, "Don't let anyone deceive you with empty words, plausible arguments, clever speech." They do affect your life. Far from gaining something through these things, you will lose something through them. Let no one deceive you, you can't do these things and not lose. So don't be deceived by plausible arguments about freedom. Don't give way to the power of propaganda. As Billy Graham said very cogently: "The new morality is simply the old immorality dressed up."

Two things are affected by these things: our future and our Father. Our future is affected in that those who do such things have no inheritance in the kingdom of God and of Christ. Don't let anybody fool you. Don't let anybody tell you that you won't lose by these things, that you can do them and get away with it – there is no inheritance. Your future is affected and lost through this. Secondly – not a *thing* but a *person*, our Father, is affected. Paul makes it quite clear that it is this kind of thing that makes our Father angry. It is because of these things that the wrath of God comes on sons of disobedience. Therefore, don't let anybody say it doesn't affect anybody else what you do with your life. It affects your future, it affects your Father in heaven, and it makes him angry. What is the alternative? The alternative is to say, "I'm not going to imitate other people; I'm going to imitate God. I'm going to copy him; I'm going to model my life on his." What will happen then? Instead of disobedience, your life will be a life of love – be imitators of God and walk in love. Walking is not very spectacular; it will be just one step at a time, as I have said. Love is concerned not with one big grand gesture but with one step after another of loving people. Now I have told you that the thing that ties together immorality, impurity, and covetousness is the desire to grab and to get. If you imitate God, your desire will be the opposite – a desire to give. No longer getting but giving; no longer selfishness, but sacrifice – be imitators of God and walk in love as Christ loved you and gave himself as a sacrifice. That is the kind of life that follows if you imitate God.

God does not grab, he gives. You notice that Paul says, "Be imitators of God as beloved children." I will tell you this: the more a child is loved, the more that child will imitate the one who loves them. Love is what makes children imitate. If a child does not love an elder, or is not loved by them, they are not so likely to imitate them. But if you are loved by someone, if you were loved by your parents, you wanted to be like them and unconsciously you assimilated their pattern of life – without realising it, you began to mimic them.

Have you ever seen a little boy swaggering down the road with a group of older boys trying to be like them – coughing as he smokes his first cigarette because he is wanting to imitate them and be big? Have you ever watched a little boy walking down the road with his father when his father loves him? Taking long strides to be like daddy – do you see the difference? Imitators of God as beloved children; walking in his footsteps. There is a nasty smell about some of the words I mentioned here, but God says that if you walk in love, then like Christ you will be to God a fragrant perfume. God has a sense of smell and he loves a sweet smell and love smells good to God.

Now let us look at the principle of *illumination*. If you are going to walk properly, you will need to walk in the light. Many years ago somebody tried walking in the dark through the front door of our new church building and we saw the broken glass. They weren't hurt but the glass was! But they were walking in darkness, that is why they did it. The principle is this: if you are going to walk properly, you need to walk in light. You need to see where you are going. You need to cast light around you. A dark path is a dangerous path. Paul quite simply teaches that the bad things of which he warned are darkness – and you cannot walk straight in the darkness.

Do you know that most of us, if we walked in the dark, would walk in circles? I'm told that it is because one of our legs is usually stronger than the other – especially if you are a driver. One minister in the Shetland Islands I remember, many years ago went out in a snowstorm and walked round in circles for three hours. Fortunately they found him. He thought he was heading somewhere but he wasn't. He couldn't see. He was walking in darkness. It was late at night and he just walked in circles.

Paul tells us that there is an association between good and light, and evil and darkness. It is interesting that most sin is committed at night because people don't like the light. They prefer the darkness because their deeds are evil. So they don't live during the day as God intended us to live. They go in for night life, which is against God's pattern. God gave the day to live and to work, and the night to sleep. Of course there are those who have to work at night but I am not referring to them here.

Notice that Paul doesn't say, "You used to be in the dark." He said, "You used to be darkness." He doesn't say, "You are now in the light." He says, "You are now light." It is not that you were in darkness or in light. You *were* darkness or you *are* light. This means that every one of us is either making this world a darker place or a lighter place – we can't help it. We are changing the degree of light in the world, all of us. So we are either darkness making the world a darker place or we are light, lighting it up a bit. Let us look at the two things. He says there are two things about darkness: it is unfruitful and unmentionable.

It is unfruitful—darkness never produces anything, it is the light that produces something. You can plant the seeds in your garden but it is the light that is needed to produce something from them. Darkness doesn't produce anything –

it is negative, it kills. Light produces – it is fruitful. Darkness has nothing to show for it. If you are darkness, your life will have nothing to show for it at the end – nothing at all, unproductive, unfruitful. It is also unmentionable. When we are darkness there are things that we cannot talk about – it would be a shame, it would be a disgrace; it would be embarrassing even to talk about them, says Paul – they are unmentionable, whereas the things that are done in the light can be talked about, can be part of conversation.

Look at the light. The New English Bible translates this beautifully: live like men who are at home in daylight. That is a lovely phrase. Some people have got such a hangover from the night before that when the sun rises they have to screw their eyes up. They are not at home in daylight. They just have to get through the day somehow, that when the darkness comes they can go back to their life. They are like the creatures that only come out at night. Live like men who are at home in the daylight then you will be fruitful. Light produces growing, ripening fruit. All that is good and right and true – that is what is meant by fruitfulness here. If you are going to produce what is good and right and true, you need to live in the light. As a plant needs to be in the sunlight to produce its fruit, you need to be in the light also.

The basic question is this: what does light do about darkness? For in this world we have got light and darkness side by side. There are lovely, good, right and true things in the world; there are horrible things as well – and they live side by side, they mix. What is the attitude of light to darkness? There are two things mentioned here: one that must be done and one that mustn't be done. Let us make it quite clear which is which. Number one: do not associate with those in darkness. Now that doesn't mean don't have any contact with them. They will never be saved if you have no contact. The word "associate" means to have regular company with.

Quite simply, as Paul says in 1 Corinthians 15, "Do not be deceived, bad company ruins good morals." Nothing could be clearer. A Christian cannot afford to be associated in regular company with those in darkness. He may do it with the best motives in the world. He may say, "I'm going in to try to win them." He may say, "I'm going to influence them for good." But if he is regularly in company with darkness, then he is laying himself open to something the Bible tells him is too much for him. Contact — yes; company — no.

Your company will decide so much whether you live in light or in darkness. It is very important that a Christian spends much time in company with other Christians. Do not associate with those in darkness, but rather expose them. Now here I am afraid I am going to come down quite heavily on the side of this translation: "but instead expose them." The Authorized Version has: "have no fellowship with the unfruitful works of darkness, but rather reprove them" – as if you must go and tell them they are doing wrong. Some Christians I believe have therefore been led into a misguided ministry at this point. Paul tells us quite definitely that it is not up to us to judge the outsider. God will judge them; we are rather to expose them. Does that mean that we have a protest parade and talk about them loudly? Paul here is talking about light, and light comes to the eye rather than the ear. He is talking about eyes rather than lips. The word here is "expose", and he says they will be exposed by light. The simple fact is that if there are secret things going on in darkness, the only thing you need to do is to switch a light on. You don't need to say anything — switch the light on and it is exposed. Someone has said, "I'd rather light a candle than curse the darkness" – a very appropriate saying for just now. Paul is talking about light that can be seen, not heard. He's saying "expose" and it is almost a photographic word, except that photography was not known to Paul. But what does the word "expose" mean? In photography it means: let the light shine in. The thing is changed when the light comes in. It has been exposed. Jesus said, "Let your light shine before men that they may see..." – not hear, but that they may see. When they see your goodness they will see their badness because light has this double effect. It exposes as well as shines. So Paul says, "Let your light shine." How can you let your light shine? The answer is: you have no light of your own, but light has a peculiar quality. Everything that light strikes becomes light, that is what Paul is saying here. It might be translated: When anything is exposed by the light, it becomes visible. I think it would almost be better to say anything that is exposed to the light becomes light—that is the literal translation. The moon shines there on a dark night and it exposes so much on the earth. But the moon has no light of its own at all. Where does it get its light? From the sun, but because the sun is shining on the moon, the moon is able to shine on the earth and expose the earth, and a bright moon can expose a great deal on earth. There were even some South Sea Islanders who worshipped the moon, rather on the principle that the moon came out at night when it was needed but the sun only shone during the day when it was light anyway. The poor little souls, they didn't realise that the moon just borrowed its light from the sun. It says, "Awake O sleeper and rise from the dead and Christ shall give you light" – which means if you weren't a sleeper Christian or even a dead Christian, the light of Christ would shine on you and that would reflect into your environment and you would expose the world in its darkness to the light of Christ. That is the picture here. That little quotation doesn't come from the Old Testament, doesn't come from the New Testament, but clearly it is a quotation. Where did Paul get it from? It seems from all we can discover that it is from one of the earliest Christian hymns, probably sung at baptismal services in the early church. "Arise O sleeper, awake." Wake up you Christian. Wake up. Don't be dead. Wake up and Christ will give you light. Then let that light shine and you will expose the darkness. So walk in the light. Reach up to the sunlight. You do that by seeking to learn what is pleasing to the Lord, says Paul. That is reaching after the sunlight. Seek to learn what pleases him. Don't try to please yourself, don't even try to please others – you never will – but seek to please the Lord. Then you are reaching up to the light and he will give you light and it will shine, and others will be exposed without a word. I don't think we need more Christians shouting, I think we need more Christians shining.

Let us move on to the third principle of walking: *intoxication* – if you want to get to walk straight you need to get intoxicated. Now that may sound really wrong but Paul says this here – not with alcohol, but with God. So he says, "Don't get drunk with wine but be filled with the Spirit." Funnily enough, to be intoxicated with God you can walk straight. If you get drunk with wine, that is the one thing you will not manage. A preacher who was preaching on that text began his sermon most dramatically with this sentence: "You've got to fill a man with something." We had great difficulty once getting the pump for the baptistry going. We tried everything and it just wouldn't pump water. So we sent for the man who put it in. He came and said, "Ah well, the pump needs priming. It's just full of air at the moment. It's got to be full of water, then it will start pumping" – and sure enough he got it going. Man needs priming otherwise he is just full of air. He breathes, but if he is really going to get out of himself and into real life he needs filling with something. That is why so many get drunk and that is why so many young people are taking drugs. They know they have got to be filled with something. They know they haven't the resources within themselves for life and so they need help.

They need some stimulus, they need some resources that they haven't got so they take drugs and they get drunk; they do something to get filled with something to get life.

In the Roman empire, drunkenness was common, but at least a man was trying to get out of himself when he got drunk. We used to say in the north that to get drunk was the quickest way out of Manchester on a Saturday night. The middle of Manchester among all the factories, with drizzle in the streets, was a miserable place and the quickest way out was to get drunk. There is only one snag with that and Paul calls it "dissipation". It is translated here "debauchery" but I think a closer English word might be "dissipation". The word means "wastefulness". It just throws your life away – it wastes time, it wastes money, it is foolish, careless, thoughtless, reckless, and above all it just throws away what God gave you. The word means to throw something away. Don't get drunk with wine wherein is debauchery; wherein is throwing your life away.

A film was made some years ago about an alcoholic, and very significantly the film was entitled Lost Weekend. Just lost – and that is the difficulty of getting drunk. You have lost that bit of your life; it has gone. Drugs are doing the same for many people. They are wanting life, they know they have got to be filled with something so they are getting high on this or that drug, but their life is getting lost. It is wasted; they have nothing to show for it. It is the same word used in Luke 15 of the prodigal son. He went to a far country. A little Sunday school boy once said to his Sunday school teacher, "He wasted his substance in righteous living" – but the word is not "righteous", it is "riotous". It is the same word here: wasteful living. Soon he had gone through all his dad's money and he had nothing to show for it. Those months of his life were lost. He thought he had enjoyed it at the time but they were lost. He had wasted it and he could never have it back again.

Paul is saying don't get high on drugs. That is just to lose your life, throwing it away. Rather, be wise, guided, and filled. Be wise—realise that the days are evil so you have got to rescue each day for good, otherwise it will just be evil and wasted and lost. So you have got to redeem the time, buy it up and seize the opportunity. Get another day back from God, from a life that would otherwise be wasted – that is a wise man. Secondly, seek the will of God. He has planned your life out. He knows what you can do with it. He has a plan for you that is just right for the length of your life. He knows how long it is going to be. Your life is just long enough to fulfil his plan but too short to waste any of it. So find out what the will of the Lord is and then you don't waste your life. It is tragic if you have gone after your own plans and desires for so long and suddenly wake up and realise it is all wasted and God had had a plan for you that would have used your life to the best possible advantage.

Finally, *be filled*. Verse 18 is a startling contrast and would not just occur to people today. But one of the things that was said to me about a new church building, and I took it as one of the greatest compliments, was: "The atmosphere coming in the front entrance was just like a pub." I was thrilled – this was what I longed to be said. Why do people go to the public house? Because people are relaxed and in fellowship and they are happy and there is noise and there is singing. Some people seem to want God's house to be as silent as a cemetery and think that is honouring to God. There is a place for quietness, especially at home on your own. But I was thrilled when somebody said it was just like a pub because I have talked to men who said to me, "I go to the pub because it is a much happier and easier place to go into than a church where everybody is so quiet and looking at the back of your head, because you have got to sit in the front row and they are all in the back and it is so uncomfortable." Well I want a church building to be a public house in the truest sense of the word. You know what is going to be needed for that? People who are drunk with God because they will not lose control of themselves then – but certain things will happen that happen in a pub. Tongues are loosened, feelings are released, song comes out, and so Paul says, "Don't get drunk with wine but do be filled with the Spirit and make melody and sing." That is what the church should be—filled with the Spirit. If you are going to walk then you can walk straight and you can be intoxicated with God. It was John Wesley who said, "I want a bunch of God-intoxicated men and I can turn England upside down."

The tragedy is that those of us who may never have been drunk (or if we have it was many years ago), never really got drunk with the Lord in its place. That leaves a kind of arid, cold, hard Christian life. Of course, people will make for the pub if they want a bit of fellowship. But be filled with the Spirit and sing and make melody in your hearts.

There are three sorts of song that a Christian can sing and Paul mentions all three: psalms—those are the Jewish songs, and a Christian can use them all, and that is why the book of Psalms is so precious to us. Then hymns, which means Christian songs composed by Christians. The third is a unique form: spiritual songs. Those are songs not composed by man at all but words and music composed by God and inspired directly by him. This is how Christians should be. They should sing as they walk. So much for the musical side of it, but what about the words? The words are so important. Here is a lovely little text for Christian singing. How do you sing? I'll tell you how. First of all, it's got to start deep down. Christian songs have got to start in the heart – not in the mouth, not in the throat, not even in the lungs; it has got to start in the heart. You can always tell when song is started there – making melody in your heart, that is where it starts. How far has it got to go? Well, it has to be to God but it has also got to be addressing one another.

Do you realise that some of the hymns we sing, we sing to each other? You may have noticed that. They are not all addressed to God, though most of them are. So we address one another – but what are the words to be about? Paul says: every day give thanks for everything. That is enough to sing about to your God: the content of Christian song is to be thanksgiving. Christian song gives thanks every day for everything, and what a difference that makes. Paul said earlier, "Don't let your speech be filled with dirty jokes and coarse language, rather let your lips be filled with thanksgiving." You cannot, for example, be a thankful and a covetous person at one and the same moment. It is absolutely impossible. So next time you are covetous, why not sing a hymn of thanks and see what happens? As our lips are filled with thanksgiving and praise and sing to God and thank him for all that he is, you find that these other wrong things of darkness, disobedience and dissipation filter out of your mind. That is a very practical way to deal with them.

THE CHRISTIAN'S WALK
– in the home

Read Ephesians 5:21–6:4

---

v. 21 What? Subjection (in an age of democracy!)
     Why? Fear (in an age of familiarity!)

A. HUSBANDS AND WIVES (5:22–33)

  1. Husband is head (22–24)
                           Direction does not mean dictatorship.
                           Intimacy does not mean insubordination.
  2. Wife is body (25–31)   Love must be –
                           costly; cleansing; caring; cleaving
  3. Head and body are one unit (32–33) like the Church and Christ

B. PARENTS AND CHILDREN (6:1–4)

  1. Children (1–3) What? Obedience; reverence
                    Why? Right; rewarding
  2. Parents (4)   Not goading
                    But guiding – instruction and admonition

What is the ideal form of government? This question is becoming more acute and more tense because there are more and more people having to live together on this little planet. People are saying there has got to be control, yet we want freedom. How can we keep these two in balance – law and liberty, form and freedom – and have the ideal kind of government? Now the governments of this world are divided between what we can call democracy and dictatorship. Democracy: believing that every person has a right to have a say in the government and that the people shall choose and change their government when they feel like doing so. Dictatorship, on the other hand, says no, the people are not free to choose – we are the government, we will decide what is going to be.

One can see problems with both. I am only going to deal with the problem of democracy because that is a form of government under which we live. I am going to predict that democracy is on the way out. It is already crumbling. It is vanishing. The reasons why it is crumbling are pretty obvious. When everybody is trying to have their say and everybody is trying to decide what is right and everybody is trying to govern, there are so many conflicts of interest and ideals that sooner or later there is trouble, and then anarchy and violence, as frustrated people who can't govern try to take over.

What has all this to do with our Bible study? Quite simply this: v. 21 is God's answer to the question: What is the ideal form of human government? It is a combination of leadership and responsibility. It is not God's will that everybody should try to run everything. It is not God's Word that everybody should go around talking about their rights to speak or to vote or to do this, that or the other. God has a plan of human government. Wherever more than one person have to live together, God has a plan for that group, whether small or large. It may be as small a group as the two you find in a marriage, husband and wife – or it may be a group of millions. However small or large the group, the pattern of government is always the same: God has an ideal plan to enable people to live together. That plan is that some should be responsible for the leadership of the others, and that both should be responsible to Christ. That is the real ideal plan if we could only achieve it. It is neither democracy nor dictatorship. It is something right in the middle of those two—a combination of the best of both, and yet a removal of the difficulties and dangers of both.

Democracy, in which we have lived, does not like that one bit. The word "subject" has become a nasty word. If you talk about subject people, immediately our modern democratic notions say, "They are people to be set free from that; subject people – that is all wrong. Yet God says if you are ever going to live together, somebody has got to be subject to someone else, otherwise you will have chaos, anarchy, a breakdown of human society. Therefore here Paul applies this whole principle to marriage, but before we do, we shall still range a bit wider. The subjection must also go with reverence or else it becomes a cringing subjection. The respect must be there as well as the subordination. Only then do you get a perfect balance. It must be reverence not for the person to whom you are subject but reverence for Christ who has delegated his authority to that person, and that is a very big difference from either a human democracy or a human dictatorship.

We could spend a lot of time applying this politically but I am not going to, except just to say that I think it is terribly difficult to establish democracy from the Word of God. It is also very difficult to establish totalitarian dictatorship. Neither is there. Before we move on to marriage, let us look at the church. The democratic atmosphere in which we have lived for so long now in the Western world has crept into every part of our thinking and even into the church. Where church members talk about their rights of voting or speaking or having their say, then the group breaks up and you have rows and division. Once again, God's pattern in the church is this: that Christ himself delegates his leadership to leaders whom he chooses. They are not chosen by popular vote, they are chosen by a group of the people of God getting together and saying, "Christ, to whom do you wish to delegate your leadership in this fellowship?" Having found that, then the members, for the reverence of Christ, can submit themselves to his delegated leadership—that is the pattern.

Now we come back to marriage. I have said all that to show you that I believe we have here a perfect blueprint for human society, and whether it is a tiny group of two people in a marriage or a few hundred people in a church or a few million people in a nation, God has laid down this blueprint which is perfect if only we could achieve it. But selfishness loses respect and before long we are talking about our rights instead of our responsibilities. As soon as you use the word "right" of yourself, you have stepped out of God's plan. As soon as you have used the word "responsibility" of yourself, you are stepping into it.

Therefore the Bible doesn't speak anywhere of the rights of wives or the rights of husbands, it speaks of the responsibilities of both to one another. Now we are going to look at this pattern. First of all, Paul takes the individual responsibility of wife, and then husband, and looks at them separately. Then he puts them together and looks at them as a unity. Here we have the ideal approach to their various responsibilities. I want you to notice first that *both* have responsibilities. Secondly, I want you to notice that they have *different* responsibilities. Paul does not say, "You both have the same responsibility to each other." He says, "This is yours", and, "this is yours" – and they are different. I wish we could get away from the confusion in modern debate about the varying roles of male and female as if difference of responsibility means difference of status or value. It doesn't. In God's sight, husband and wife are of equal value and equal status – they are both sinners, needing grace. But they are not of the same function and that is an entirely different thing.

So let us look at the basic principle behind all marriage. What is happening in a marriage? Are two people deciding to live together? Well it is that, but it is much more. Are they simply saying, "It'll be cheaper for us to live in one house than in two flats?" They will discover that it isn't. Are they just saying, "Well this is a respectable way to make love?" That is what marriage is in some people's minds. What are they really doing? According to God's Word, when two people get married, two people are becoming one person. The word "one" is very important in the marriage service. It is not two going to go forward together, it is two becoming one. Before they are married they have been two people with two bodies and two heads. When they have become wed, it is vital that they should reduce the number of bodies and reduce the number of heads. Can I put it this way? A two-headed marriage is a grotesque and monstrous caricature, a two-headed monster. God intends a marriage to be composed of a head and a body because it is going to be one person only from now on. Therefore, he approaches the whole matter of relationships between husband and wife on the basis that we assume we are no longer two people each with our rights, but one person. The separate responsibilities are going to make one whole person together – that is the basic understanding of Christian marriage here.

So first of all, I have to address wives. You will notice that the husbands have much more said to them than the wives do. So I will say more to the husbands and for other reasons too. But the first basic thing is this: from now on there is one head and one body making one person. The husband is to be the head and the wife is to be the body. In that kind of partnership they will be able to make one new person. Therefore, the varying responsibilities are these: wives treat your husband as your head; husbands, treat your wives as your body, and then you will discover how to live together in God's will.

We will explore in greater detail what this means. I find the tremendous challenge here: wives, imagine that you are married to Jesus and behave accordingly – that is what Paul says. Imagine that your husband is Jesus and you behave towards him exactly as you would to the Lord. I am paraphrasing but I am not putting to you anything that isn't in the scripture. "Wives be subject to your husband as to the Lord." Now this may seem almost a blasphemous thought to some, and maybe a little irreverent, but I want you wives to imagine that it was Jesus who fell in love with you and proposed to you and asked you to marry him. How would you feel towards him? He never did propose to anybody, he never did get married while he was on earth. The answer was that he was coming to seek a different bride and he is going to be married and so Jesus knows what it is to fall in love and want a bride and seek to protect her and sacrifice for her. But wife, imagine that you are married to Jesus. Now it may be that your husband is not very Christ-like, but it is still your duty to behave as if he were Christ. That is a remarkable attitude. It means that you have got a very simple test for any action or attitude towards him, and the simple test is: if I were married to Jesus, would I be saying this? Would I be doing this? Would I be behaving like this?

That is a very simple yardstick by which you can judge your own attitude. You have even got another standard to help you to judge. Look at the church. How does the church behave towards Christ? Then you behave the same way. Did you ever hear a church arguing with Christ? Did you ever hear a church answering back to Christ? Did you ever hear a church trying to tell Christ what to do? Maybe you say, "Yes I did." Well, it wasn't a true church. The pattern that wives are to adopt to their husbands is the attitude that the church should have to Christ. For the church is Christ's bride, and Christ said: I am the bridegroom. The pattern of relationship is very clearly there. Christ's plan is always that the leadership in the marriage should be in the husband – always, as it is always his will that the leadership of the church should be in Christ's hands and not vice-versa. Nothing spoils marriage so quickly as a wife who has come to look down on her husband instead of looking up to him. Girls who are not married yet, if you are thinking of marriage, don't marry a man you can't look up to. Don't say, "Well I can reform him." Don't say, "I can make a man of him." Don't say, "I can lift him up; I can improve him." You are starting on the wrong foot. You can't respect a man while that is your attitude. Wait for a man who will lift you up, a man who can improve you, and then marry him. Otherwise you can't look up to his leadership, and sooner or later you will say, "I'm a better Christian than he is. I have more willpower than he has. I am better at mixing with people than he is." I have heard wives say this, and my heart has sunk because it means they are no longer looking up to the one they married. So find a man you can look up to, not a man you think needs improving. All men need improving (myself included) but a wife shouldn't start off by saying, "I'm the one to do it." Rather she should say, "I marry him because I look up to him and I respect him and I want him to lead me." So much for wives.

At this point I want to meet a very common criticism of

what Paul has to say. People say that Paul, in telling wives to be subject to their husbands, is simply reflecting the social customs of his day, that this is a typical attitude towards women of two thousand years ago, that you find it among Jews, you find it among Greeks, and you find it among Romans. They all talked about the rights of the husband and the responsibilities of the wife and it is one-sided and we are not going to stand for it and we are in women's lib and all that.

I want to point out that Paul's teaching is completely different from the social standards of his day, and I will tell you why. He goes on to say the husband has responsibilities. You don't find that anywhere in Greek or Roman society. You find that they did say the wife has responsibilities but the husband has none. He has his rights and he can treat his wife like that, and that is where it went wrong and that is where Jesus introduced a totally new attitude. He taught that it is not only those who follow who have a responsibility, those who lead have responsibilities too – and that puts the whole thing in a completely different light. It alters the whole picture. So much more is said to husbands than to wives. Husbands have the greater responsibility because they have been called to lead. In the Bible, it is always the leader who carries the heavier accountability to God. Now let us look at the husband's duties. If your wives are going to imagine that they are married to Christ, you husbands will not have to stretch that imagination too far. I think you understand what I am meaning. You must make it easy for them to imagine they are married to Christ. In other words, you must be to them what Christ would be. Otherwise you cannot blame them if they have difficulty accepting your leadership. In other words, if they are going to submit to you, it must be because you have submitted to Jesus. Otherwise you have no right. It is possible for some people to take the

Bible teaching and use it as an excuse for a petty dictatorship within the marriage and say, "I've got Bible authority to boss you." I think the wife has authority to reply: "... and Christ has biblical authority to boss you" – though I don't think that would just be the wisest way to do it. But you might ask somebody else to say that to him.

But a husband ought to have towards his wife an attitude exactly the same as Christ has to the church. If the wife should model herself on the church's attitude to Christ, the husband should model himself on Christ's attitude to the church. That means, in one word, love. A wife doesn't mind submitting to one who loves her deeply. She wants that; she wants to be able to trust and to respond to a leader who loves, so that neither democracy nor dictatorship is the pattern for marriage. Democracy comes unstuck because you can't get a majority vote. If each of you says, "I have a right to my say," you have reached a complete impasse. Dictatorship doesn't work either because the husband then rides roughshod over the wife. But what kind of love is in mind? – the kind of love that Christ has for all of us, and I will tell you what kind of a love that is.

First of all, it is a love that is prepared to make any sacrifice, even the ultimate one. It is a love that doesn't count the cost. It is a love that is not calculating. It's a love that says, "I will give anything for my beloved, even my life." If a wife feels that her husband loves her that much, not just a few petty gifts, but the biggest gift of all, prepared to give himself to his wife, then she will submit gladly and eagerly and lovingly herself, but that is a very costly love. It costs more than an occasional bunch of flowers. To give yourself is a very big gift to give and we men are selfish and we can keep ourselves to ourselves. I would be a wealthy man if I had a fifty-pound note for every wife who has said, "My husband doesn't talk to me." To talk to someone is to give yourself and that is part of this costly love.

The second thing about Christ's love is that it is always a cleansing love. It leaves a person better than they were before the love began. So Christ loved his church and gave himself for her that he might wash her, cleanse her, sanctify her, make her better. He wanted, like every husband, a beautiful bride without spot or wrinkle or any blemish to spoil the beauty. How a bride wants to be beautiful for her husband. But in a sense, it is the husband who is often responsible for his wife's beauty. She may have had glamour or good looks beforehand but beauty is what we are talking about now. A husband is largely responsible for the beauty of his wife. It is his job to create in her and to help her to be the kind of person whose beauty of character will transform the face and shine out.

Let us go a little further. Paul says quite bluntly that you husbands before you married looked after your own body – didn't you? You fed it, you clothed it, you nourished it, you cherished it, you looked after yourself. Paul is saying: now that you have married, look after your wife as you used to look after your own body, because she is now your body. Nourish, cherish – notice that the second word goes way beyond the first. "Nourish" means give the necessities; "cherish" means add the extras. Again, this is how Christ treats his church. He doesn't just give us the necessities. He loves us so he cherishes us. It is the extras that are going to show how much you love.

So far I have mentioned individual responsibilities – the wife and the husband. Now we see them together as an integrated relationship. So far we have been looking at two people but now Paul quotes Genesis 2:24, "A man shall leave his father and mother and cleave to his wife and the two shall become one." For purposes of responsibility you have got to think of wife and husband separately. For purposes of understanding what has happened, you think of them together. Now this verse in Genesis contains within it two meanings – a physical meaning and a spiritual meaning. Paul has seen both.

Take first the physical meaning: marriage has two sides. It is a breaking of some relationships and a making of others. It is a leaving and a cleaving, and that is why at a certain point a minister taking a traditional service says, "Who gives this woman to be married to this man?" A voice says, "I do," and it is neither bride nor groom but the bride's father. Do you know, weddings are sad occasions as well as glad? I have noticed that the tears and laughter are very close together because, in a sense, the relationships are changing. There is a breaking; a leaving. There is a break up of one family, two families in fact, to make one new one. The parents are bound to feel that. It is a time when, in a sense, the relationships are being eased off because they are going to need the chance to build a new family together. There would not be nearly as many jokes about mothers-in-law if this were fully realised – that there is a leaving to make the cleaving, and there has got to be that break.

This is the physical side, the leaving and the cleaving. You are leaving a relationship in which you learned love and you are going to create a new circle in which that can be multiplied and passed on. Some people say to me, "Why do you need a marriage ceremony if two young people love each other? Why can't they just go and live together and intend to stay together and just get on their knees and promise before God that they are going to be husband and wife? Why do they have to come to church? Why do they have to have a ceremony?" – Precisely because it is leaving as well as cleaving. It is not just a relationship between the two of them, it is going to affect a lot of other people and this must be openly recognised. It is a social contract. Marriage is not just a young man cleaving to his wife; it is a young man leaving his father and mother, and that is being recognised. In society, the two young people have left their homes – they haven't just decided to start a new home together. They have left their old homes and it is a public recognition of others that the leaving has taken place. (Please refer to my book *Remarriage is Adultery Unless...* for a discussion of the issue of divorce and remarriage.)

For the Christian marriage, as I have already pointed out, not even death parts us. For though in heaven we are neither married nor given in marriage, nevertheless we shall enjoy a closer, deeper, more wonderful relationship with each other in glory than we could ever know on earth. The difference will be that whereas on earth the relationship between husband and wife is an exclusive one that they cannot share with others – it is too intimate and sacred and it must be kept between them – in heaven the relationship will be shared with the whole bride, all of the church, and we shall enjoy perfect love.

This has not been an easy passage to study. It is so practical, so down-to-earth, it is so clear, and this is God's pattern for all our society, whether it is the large groups of nations or communities or the tiny group of a marriage. We shall move on to see the same pattern in the family, the leadership of parents, the submission of children as in the Lord. We shall look at our relationships at work between employer and employee, and we will find the same pattern. For written over all human relationships is God's pattern for government: Be subject to one another out of reverence for Christ.

6:1–4
We are now going to look at God's pattern for the family. Once again, the same principle applies: leadership and

loyalty. You cannot run a family as a democracy in which everybody in the family has an equal vote and an equal say. Neither can you run the family as a dictatorship in which children are treated like robots or machines or worse. The pattern is leadership and loyalty. We are going to look at the kind of loyalty that children should have and the kind of leadership that parents should exercise.

The Bible does not talk about the rights of the children or the rights of the parents; it talks about the responsibilities of the children and the responsibilities of the parents. Then you can build a happy family for God. Within this framework, I believe that children will have the one thing that many of them miss today: security. We know that the majority of crimes committed by juveniles go back to insecurity in the home. They do not feel safe or secure within the framework of the family, often because there is no framework, no ordered pattern. This produces within children a deep feeling of insecurity which comes out in tantrums and rebellion. Children want to know where they are.

Now I am not going to try to be a child psychologist. I am afraid that I am a bit like the man who said that he started life with six theories as to how to bring up children. He finished life with six children and no theories. It ill behoves any of us, I think, to hold ourselves up as an example. But I am going to explain the Word of God to you. We begin with the framework of the family as seen on the children's side – the kind of loyalty that children should have toward parents – that is their responsibility. The children are addressed directly by the Bible, they are therefore old enough to listen.

They are old enough to have listened to the whole of Paul's letter to the Ephesians. They won't have understood it all; not even adults understand it all at the first reading, but they are children addressed as responsible people. They are told two things: one concerned with their actions and the other concerned with their attitudes – obedience and reverence. You can have one without the other, but God's will for the child or the youth is both.

"Obedience" is a word that is dropping out of the English language. When did you last hear it used in ordinary conversation? In its place is coming a horrible word "self-expression", as if the most important thing for a child is to express itself. God does not talk about self-expression in his Word, he talks about obedience. The word he uses here for obedience is an extraordinary one which means literal obedience to the letter. Consider the shortest story Jesus ever told: "A man had two sons, and he went to the first and said, 'Son, go and work in the vineyard today,' and he answered, 'I will not.' But afterward he repented and went. He went to the second son and said the same, and he answered, 'I will go, sir,' but did not go. Which of the two did the will of his father?" That is the simplest and the plainest story that Jesus ever told. Those who argue that the Bible can be interpreted in a lot of ways ought to start with that story. I don't know of more than one interpretation for it. You notice the father didn't say to the son, "Please, will you go and work in the farm?" He said, "Go and work in the farm today." The son said, "I will," and he didn't. The simple lesson of that simple story is obedience. The amazing thing is that Jesus was the perfect example. When should a child stop being obedient to parents? At what age? At what age should you say to them, "You're on your own now"? Well we used to say twenty-one; now we say eighteen. It is climbing down all the time. The law follows the trend; the trend is usually well below the legal age. But a Jewish boy was considered "grown up" at twelve. From the age of twelve he made his own decisions, and he was responsible for keeping the law. Up to that point his parents were responsible if he broke the law, but after that, the boy was.

The most amazing thing one reads about the life of Jesus is that at the age of twelve he went back to Nazareth and was subject to Mary and Joseph. He could have said, "I'm grown up now. I have come of age. You have no right to tell me what to do." Yet over and above the age at which he could have been free, Jesus gave a profound example to every teenager today. He was subject to his parents – not very popular teaching this, but it is there.

Why should you obey your parents? The answer – there is only one reason – is that it is right. You notice it doesn't say, "Because it pays." It may pay; it may not. Because it is right. That is a word that is dropping out of the English language too – just to do a thing because it is right. Youngsters today say, "I want reasons; you will have to explain to me why it is right." But God says obey your parents because it is right. There is no other reason needed than that it is right.

You notice that one of the boys of the two in the parable was obedient, but not very happily. He didn't want to do it; he said, "No," but he did it. That was better than the lad who said, "I'll do it," and didn't do it. But better still is the boy who says, "I will" and does it. For to obedience he has added reverence. To the action he has added an attitude.

Why Paul quotes God's commandment concerning honouring your father and mother is this: it is God's will for children not only that they should obey, but that they should willingly and honourably obey. You can obey very reluctantly because your father is bigger than you are and because you could not argue with him. Or you could obey gladly because you honour your father as a wiser person than you are, as a better person than you are, as someone who has been around more corners than you have, as someone who has seen more of life than you have, and you know he wouldn't tell you to do this unless it was good, and that is a different kind of obedience. It is a respect for the parents' position and age and advice, which again is singularly rare as a virtue today. Instead, there are epithets. The word "father" is not used so much. There is "the old man", and that is a rather critical phrase when you look at it. Epithets like this erode and nibble at a respect – which we have to think about. Obedience with reverence – that is doing the will of your parents because you do look up to them and not down on them. "Honour" means to look up to someone.

God thought this commandment so important that it was the first and the only one of the Ten Commandments to which he attached a promise. The promise was that (other things being equal) your health and your wealth will be improved by honouring your parents. Since that promise is repeated in the New Testament, I take it quite literally for Christians as well as Jews that your health and your wealth will be better, other things being equal, if you learn this attitude toward your parents. I have lived long enough now to see the truth of this promise. That does not mean that if you honour your parents you are going to be a millionaire. It does mean that you will be wealthier than if you grew up a rebellious child and if you grew up centred on yourself. The word "health" includes not only physical health but mental and emotional health, and again I have lived long enough to see also that, very often, it is in the homes where this does not happen that you get emotional ill-health – where there is a bad relationship between fathers and children you get problems later.

This is the first part of God's will for the family in chapter 6. Children, you have a double duty to your parents: obedience and reverence. Or to use another word that has died right out of the English language, obedience and obeisance – they are related words. The first means to do what you are told; the second means to do it because you respect the one who told you.

Now let me turn to the other side. It is easy enough to throw that bit of the book at your children, but there is a fourth verse, and we must look at it now as parents. If we are going to expect this kind of loyalty from our children, we must give the kind of leadership to our children that God has told us to give. In other words, how can children honour parents who are not honourable? You are imposing a strain on the children that is very great, and since you are the older and the mature and the responsible one in the partnership, it is up to you to give them the encouragement to give you the loyalty. To be honoured, then, parents need to be honourable.

I notice that v. 4 is addressed to the fathers. Mothers can take a rest now. Why should God address fathers? There are two reasons. Number one comes out of our study of the previous chapter: the father is the head of the house and he is ultimately responsible for the standards of discipline and behaviour in the house. There is something wrong when a mother has to decide all the questions of discipline and has to tell the children what standards are right and what are wrong. But there is another reason. I have not yet met a mother who didn't have some natural instinct to protect and guide and care for a child. But I have met many fathers who did not have that instinct. Somehow, and I confess it, our male nature is such that we do not find it as easy or as natural to take our part in the family life as a mother does, which is why in the typical British family it is the mother who brings up the children rather than the father – and that is not God's will. Matriarchal society is not the pattern of our Creator but we fathers are not so good at it. We are far more likely than the mothers to fail in our responsibility toward the children, so I address fathers now, and those who will be fathers.

First of all, we are told something we mustn't do. "Do not prick," that's the literal word, "do not prick your children."

Do not provoke anger, irritate, goad. I think "goad" is the best word. Literally, when a man was ploughing in the Middle East, he had his oxen in front. He had a long stick about six or seven feet long, and at the end of it was a spike. The way he kept his oxen ploughing when they were getting tired was to keep pricking them. You may see it to this day in the Middle East – goading, pricking – and that is precisely the word used here. It is the word used of Saul of Tarsus on the Damascus Road. God said, "It's hard for you to kick against the pricks," and it is the same word. Fathers, you won't get anywhere for constantly prodding your children from behind. That is not the way to do it. Paul goes on to say in Colossians that if you do this, they will be discouraged. I suppose one of the greatest crimes a father can commit is to discourage his children rather than encourage them.

Let us enlarge on this a bit. How do you prick them? Well, I will tell you one or two ways that we can do it. We can be over-strict. If we are over-strict, we are always telling them not to do things. A little boy at school, when asked his name, said, "My name is Johnny Don't."

The teacher said, "Surely not."

"Well," he said, "that's what dad always calls me." Now you can understand the problem here. That is goading – aggravating and irritating.

Another way is constant, carping criticism, and that can be very discouraging. I think we have got the message, we fathers: Do not goad your children. It builds up resentment and sooner or later, there will be a blow back. Sooner or later, the safety valve will blow. You will be confronted with your own child defying and shouting at you, and you will wonder how it ever came to happen. You will blame the child, and in fact, you have just been goading them so much that finally they burst.

Well now, what should we do? There are two words Paul

uses translated in the Bible "discipline" and "instruction". They are both surprisingly negative words. I mean by this that both of them are related to wrongdoing. One word means to deal with it in deed and the other to deal with it in word. Let us take the first: admonition or discipline in the Bible simply means punishment. A child psychologist was asked, "Should there be a place for corporal punishment?" – and she replied, "Yes, if you have a definite end in view." You can take that how you like. The Bible most certainly has a place for corporal punishment – not a lot, but it does say, "Spare the rod and spoil the child." It was God who said that first. Here are just a few verses from Hebrews 12:

My son, do not regard lightly the discipline of the Lord nor lose courage when you are punished by him. For the Lord disciplines him whom he loves and chastises every son whom he receives. It is for discipline that you have to endure. God is treating you as sons. For what son is there whom his father does not discipline? If you are left without discipline, in which all have participated, then you are illegitimate children and not sons. Besides this, we have had earthly fathers to discipline us, and we respected them. Shall we not much more be subject to the Father of spirits and live? For they disciplined us for a short time at their pleasure, but he disciplines us for our good that we may share his holiness.

What does "at their pleasure" mean? Very often a human father administers pain to a child to work off his own feelings. God never does that, he does it always for our good, that we might share his holiness, but the discipline is there. Have you never known the discipline of the Lord and the chastisement of the Lord and how he has brought you back to himself through pain? As Hebrews says, it may have been a painful experience at the time, but afterwards you were very thankful for it.

The word "discipline" means to cause pain of some kind to a child because you love them. I used to laugh at those who said, "This hurts me more than it does you." I now know that if you love someone, it does. It hurts God to discipline us; it will hurt us to discipline our children. With the admonition or punishment must go verbal instruction as to why you did it, and this is the vital thing. Punishment without instruction is inadequate. To punish a child and not tell them why you did it will just leave the child in a situation of pain, resentment and hatred. But it is vital if you are going to punish that you add instruction. Say, "Do you know why I did that?" Take an example: one of the things that must be dealt with very firmly indeed is dishonesty. You will never have to teach your child to be dishonest; you will only have to teach them to be honest. You will never have to teach your child to tell lies; you will only have to teach your child to tell the truth.

All the Bible teaching assumes that a child's nature is basically bad and will need correction if it is to become good. This runs contrary to modern belief that basically human nature is good. The Christian doesn't believe that. We believe in God; we believe in Jesus, but we do not believe in men. We can't, because we know our own hearts and the more we are revealed to ourselves, the nearer we come to Jesus, the more we say, "In me there is no good thing." You have passed on to your children the nature with which you were born. One of the most disturbing things about having children is to see your own faults coming out in them and to realise that you didn't bring a little innocent child into the world. You brought a child who could say with King David, "In sin my mother conceived me." She gave me the nature I have, and so did my father – and we did. That which is born of the flesh is flesh, which is why it is vital that we pray that our children be born of the Spirit. Therefore, discipline and instruction go together.

What is your reaction to all this? Our first reaction is to feel this is terribly old-fashioned teaching; that this is Victorian. It isn't, it goes back longer than that – much longer. It goes way back to the Bible days. It goes way back to God in heaven. He planned it all, and I plead with parents to realise what we are at last beginning to see, that young people desperately need guidelines. They desperately need the security of being given some direction as to what is right and what is wrong. If there are no fences, they do not even know when they trespass. To bring up a child without punishment or prohibition would be to bring up a deprived child.

Who is sufficient for these things? I think one of the reasons we shrink from all this is that, knowing our own hearts, we know that anger and frustration and selfishness in the parent's heart spoils the discipline. We spank because we are annoyed, not for the good of the child. Knowing how easily we abuse our responsibility, we shrink back. Or else, knowing how often we have sinned, we say, "Well, we must overlook it in them because we've overlooked it in ourselves." Who is sufficient?

I thank God that he not only gave us a plan for family life but a person to help us. He didn't just say, "This is the routine; this is the regulation. This is the pattern." He will help us. Children, obey your parents in the Lord. Parents, discipline your children with the admonition of the Lord – and that is the real answer to it. If the Lord Jesus Christ is in the discipline, if he is in the obedience, if the Lord Jesus Christ is a vital part of the family, then these things cease to be thought of as old-fashioned, and they are seen to be as the right way to conduct family life.

THE CHRISTIAN'S WALK
– at work

Read Ephesians 6:5–9

A. EMPLOYEES (5–8)

What?   Respectful obedience
Conscientious loyalty
Cheerful service

Why?   Regarded by the Lord
Rewarded by the Lord

B. EMPLOYERS (9)

What? Not exploitation
But consideration

Why?   Power of the Lord
Punishment of the Lord

Here is one of the most practical subjects: your daily work. Paul is quite ruthless in applying the principles of the Christian faith to every department of life. He will not allow us to keep Christ in a little chapel, so to speak, as if we can make a special little room in our life just for Christ and keep him there and go and meet him there, and then go into the other rooms and do what we like. If he is not Lord of all, he is not Lord at all. Paul has been applying this to various parts of our life: to marriage, to family life, to the use of leisure and our fun, to our church relationships. Now he comes right down to that part of our life which occupies most of our waking hours.

If you don't see Christ in your work and use it for him, do you realise that you are probably going to waste at least half of your waking life? If we can only serve Christ in our leisure time, then most of us will lose many hours that he gave us. To put it another way: perhaps not all, but most Christians have most relationships with unbelievers at work. It is there that they will need to let their light shine before men. Notice that light is something that goes to the eyes, not the ears. In fact, at work people ought to *see* your Christianity. It is not right to use the boss's time to be witnessing to everybody in the office all day, though I am sure there are some moments when the Lord tells you it has got to be done. But for the normal routine, our light has to be seen.

Christianity changed people's attitude to work as much as any other attitude. We have seen already how Christ changed people's attitude to women and to children and to widows and to orphans, but he changed people's ideas of work quite radically. For Christ came into a world in which people did not like work and they did not want to work. Their ambition was to stop work and it was every man's ambition to be able to afford a slave to do his work for him.

A slave cost thirty pieces of silver – that was the price of status. If you could get thirty pieces of silver, you could buy a slave and you could get him to do your work and you were free to enjoy leisure, culture and every pursuit that you liked. It is interesting that Judas bargained for the life of Jesus for the price of a slave, presumably that he might buy one and be free not to work. But in Greek and Roman society, one out of every three did not work; two out of every three were slaves and did the work. Every doctor was a slave, every teacher was a slave. These days have gone. We now have immigrants. Our hospitals would close down if we did not rely on immigrant labour to keep them going, and a new pattern is coming. Indeed, we now live in a society that is increasingly going back to the days of the Roman Empire when it was corrupt and decaying and on its last legs. One of the symptoms of a sick society is more money, less work, more leisure.

The new attitude to work which Christianity brought to light is based on the fact that God works. Not all the time — six-sevenths of the time God works, and man, made in the image of God, will find that if he does the same he will find a truer fulfilment.

Genesis 2 says, "When God had finished his work, he had a rest." He said, "Let us make man in our own image." This is the pattern for man: that he works and rests and finds in that his true fulfilment.

When Jesus came, he was a worker. We need to remember that although he spent three years in full-time service, if you don't mind my putting it that way, he spent eighteen years in a shop working with his hands. The Son of God — eighteen years in the shop, three years saving souls. Again, Jesus gave a pattern for a fulfilled life and we often forget the eighteen years. The Holy Spirit, too, is a worker and seems, at times, to be the busiest of all three persons of the Godhead – always busy doing something. Jesus said, "My Father worked until now. Now I am working."

Work is a vital part of the Christian life. Therefore, Christians say two things about work. One: Christians have upheld the plain *duty* of work. The Bible doesn't say your work has to be pleasant, congenial to your personality, easy. It says your work has to be done well – that is all. "Six days shall you labour." Indeed, this principle is taken so seriously, that Paul says in one of his letters: "If a Christian refuses to work when he could, then you must not give him a meal; it's the only way to teach him." One of the disturbing features of the great wave of Christian interest among young people today is that there is one wing of it that is saying, "Drop your job; don't work, just go out and preach—that is all you've got to do." But that is not true to the whole teaching of the New Testament. Paul said, "If a man will not work, neither shall he eat." It is the duty of every Christian to work.

Secondly, the Bible teaches the *dignity* of work. We don't have to have a job that is dignified. Any job may be dignified if it is done for Christ. Therefore, it is interesting that both Jesus and the man who wrote this letter, Paul, though they both had brilliant minds, and I am speaking humanly here, they both could have chosen work that meant that they need not work with their hands at all. They could both have been philosophers at a human level; they could both have been lecturers – Paul had had university education – but both of them worked with their hands and set an example to people to teach us that there is a dignity of manual labour.

There is not only a dignity of manual labour in the Bible; there is a dignity of menial tasks. Do you know what was the dirtiest job reserved for the lowest slave in the household in the ancient world? The dirtiest job of all was to wash smelly feet. Even the slaves refused to do it; it was the bottom slave, the youngest and the newest slave in the house, who had to wash feet of hot travellers, tired from a journey. One day, Jesus took a towel and he girded himself and knelt down and he washed smelly feet. He said, "Do you know what I've just done? I've given you an example." There is no task too menial or too manual to have the dignity of the Lord upon it.

Well now, it is against that background that we must ask: "What is the meaning of the word 'vocation' when it's applied to our daily work?" I have had many people come to see me over my years of ministry who have said, "I've come because I want to apply my Christianity to my job; I want to bring Christ into my work." That is a very fine thing to come and talk over, but then they have always gone on to say, "So I'm asking, what job I should be doing?" That is the wrong question. Our vocation is not what job should we be doing, but how should we be doing the job we have got. If a man is a road sweeper, then his vocation is not to drop everything and go off as a missionary, but to be a Christian road sweeper and to do it for the glory of God. I mention it because I knew a Christian road sweeper. He lived in a northern town and every morning he went into a Church of England parish church, leant his brush and shovel up against the communion rail, and prayed for his work. So this is the real question. Your work is a vocation, not because of what you do, but because of how you do it – and that is a very different matter. In all the conversations and interviews I have had discussing with people how to apply Christianity to their job, I have never had one who asked, "How may I do my job to the Lord's glory?" It has always been, "What job should I do?"

So, basically, Christ is more interested in how we do our job than in what we do. You wouldn't have chosen the task of carpenter for the Son of God, would you? Only God could make such a choice. It is such an ordinary, down-to-earth thing. What a waste of his personality and talents for eighteen years! But I know that Jesus made a square door and a chair that didn't rock, and he served the Father for those eighteen years. It was how he did it, I am quite sure, that mattered rather than what he did.

If it should be that the Lord wants you in something else, then he must make it clear; he must throw you out of the job you are doing. It must not be sought because you don't like the job you are doing – he must throw you out of it into something else. But I suppose that all of us, when we became Christians, wanted to work in a Christian office or we wanted to drop everything and be a missionary, and yet God would say start where you are. How you do your job brings into the picture attitudes and relationships. Most of us work with other people. I have the doubtful advantage of being self-employed so I have got to be both employer and employee. I have got to listen to both things that Paul says here. But most people work with others and that involves relationships and attitudes, and this is what Paul is concerned about.

Before we look at the details, let us recall the context. All this business started way back at 5:21, "Be subject to one another". It is that theme that he applies to marriage, to parents and children, to employer and employee. Paul is going to say there must be leadership and loyalty. This will only work if both sides think of their responsibilities rather than their rights. One of the things that is bedevilling industrial relations and lies behind so many battles at the industrial level is that people think of their rights rather than their responsibilities. Attitudes and relationships are behind so many of the troubles we have. You take a factory where relationships are good – and strikes are down and production is up. But take a factory where relationships are bad and attitudes are wrong, and it is one trouble after another. Paul is putting his finger right on it here when he shows us that it is not the work you do, it is the way you do it. So he speaks first to employees, those who work for others. To them he says not a word about time or money, as if to say that must not be your first concern as Christians. There are three verses now which one would love to expound at the annual Assembly of the Trade Union Congress, just as there is a verse later that we could take to the Chamber of Commerce or whatever is the equivalent of the other group. What should an employee do at work? How should they behave? What is their attitude? Three things: respectful obedience, conscientious loyalty and cheerful service – and those three find most of us out.

Respectful obedience means doing what you are told to do and doing it with the heart and not just the hand. This means not saying, "I know how to do it better than he who has told me. I'm sure I can find another way to do it." The kind of respect Paul means is this: that you really do believe that the person who told you what to do knows better than you do, and accept that, and do it as he told you. Now that is quite a rub to some people who find it very difficult to do a job just as they have been told to do it. But what a joy it is when somebody can be relied on to complete a job as they have been told to do it.

Paul says that is the first thing people should see. "With fear and trembling" – now that sounds a bit strong and some may have a little difficulty having fear and trembling at work. It doesn't mean terror, abject cringing, it means that kind of reverence, the fear of doing it wrongly, the fear that makes you take care over it. Trembling, lest you be on the mat and have it pointed to you, "That job is badly done and is not done in the way you were told." That is a situation Christians shouldn't find themselves in.

The second thing: *conscientious loyalty*. We used to have a word in the RAF: "skiving". It is a very difficult word to define. It means to appear to be in one place when actually you are in another; or to appear to be working when, actually, you haven't done a stroke of work. It really can be reduced to a fine art. Some men in the forces were absolute past masters at it – the skill that can be developed in just sheer skiving! Paul is saying here: "No skiving." You don't just work when the boss is around or when the foreman is looking. You remember that there is someone's eye upon you all the time. Even if the boss is away, somebody is there. I have to remind myself of that from time to time. Nobody is watching me, so I must remember that Somebody is.

The third thing is *cheerful service*. That does not just mean grinning service, it means, "Yes, I'll do that," not, "All right, if you insist", or, "Well, I've got too much on anyway," but, "Yes, I'll do that" – a cheerful worker; cheerful service. Do you notice how often Paul uses the word "heart"? Work starts in the heart. It is maybe a thing of the hands or the head, but it starts with the heart. He talks about, "Is your heart in it?" He talks about doing it with a will. Isn't that an interesting expression – working with a will? Nehemiah got the wall of Jerusalem built because the people had a mind to work; they got on with it.

Many years ago I saw a varied group of men putting a church building up. Very quickly it stood out which ones had a mind to work; which men would cheerfully say, "Yes, I'll do that"; which men responded to a suggestion and were ready to be told; which just went on and did it their own way, to whom it had to be said: "Look, we asked you to do this and it's not done like that." What a difference it was and how much more quickly and cheaply a building could be put up, if all were in the first category. Paul is saying to Christians: let your light shine before men.

It will not always be easy. If you are working harder than the others then you may have the shop steward after you. There are all kinds of problems today. A bricklayer once had the problem that he knew if he did a fair day's work he could lay more bricks than the other workmen were supposed to lay. What was he to do? That is the kind of problem a Christian has to wrestle with God in prayer over and work out. It is not an easy one. He may have to pay very heavily for doing what the Lord tells him to do, but servants, this is your way.

Why? Two reasons, one of which I have mentioned: your work is regarded by the Lord. There is always an eye on you and it is the Lord watching. If you do that, you do it not as men pleasers, eye service, but because God is watching and it has got to be good enough for him. Secondly, because you will be rewarded by the Lord; there may be no more in your pay packet at the end of the week or month, but there will be more treasure in heaven at the end of the day. We shall be rewarded by the Lord – you will never get God in your debt. You will always get your wages there. God will owe no man anything.

So, in a sense, Paul has given us a delightful incentive. Some people say you should not have incentives, you should not need a reward. Jesus knew human nature and he encouraged us with rewards. He said, "Great is your reward in heaven." It is just that you will have to wait a bit longer for it. You may not get your wages on earth, but you will get them. Listen, he will receive the same again from the Lord whether he is a slave or free. The significance of that is a slave got no wages at all, but a Christian slave says, "I'm going to get wages." What a difference! Somehow it puts the whole thing on a new basis. In other words, I am now employed by the Lord. I am not saying that as a minister but for you too. I am now employed for the Lord and I will be paid by the Lord. That is how I am going to work, and that makes all the difference.

Now let us turn to the employers, and v. 9 is a revolution. In the Roman and Greek world, a slave owner had no responsibility whatsoever for his slave. If the slave broke a cup and saucer while washing up, the master was free to put him to death. A slave had no rights – therefore the owner had no responsibilities. The master could do anything he liked with his slave. He was simply a tool, and when the tool was sick or useless, he could be discarded or destroyed. It is a terrible picture that emerges from the picture of Roman and Greek slavery.

Paul was teaching this: you slave owners have a responsibility for your slave. You must treat them in the same way that I have said they must treat you: as people, no longer as things. In the early days of the Industrial Revolution, men and women in England were called "hands". A man would be asked, "How many hands have you in your factory?" not, "How many people?" Nowadays we might say heads, but Paul is telling masters, employers: your employees are people, therefore you must not exploit them and you must not treat them in such a way that terror is the weapon that you have over their heads. There have been employers and situations where men were held in terror for their families, in terror of unemployment, in terror of things that could be done to them. Paul is saying that threats are out – not exploitation, but consideration.

Why? First of all, remember the power of the Lord. Remember that you are employed also. You may be at the top of your firm; you may be the highest executive officer, the managing director, but remember that you have a master. This would change board meetings, and it does. I thank God that there are some firms in this country where the top person acknowledges that he is an employee of the Lord. I think of many who would say, "I am not at the top; I am still below someone." Because of that, they can apply their Christian faith to their employees.

Attitudes and relationships are a vital factor. Remember the power of the Lord, and remember the Roman centurion who said, "I also am a man under authority, therefore I say to this man, 'Do this', and he does it." An employer who says, "I am under the authority of the Lord", will be a man who can say, "Do this," and it is done. To be under authority is to be in authority. It is in the arbitrary dictatorship of the man who thinks he is the great "I am" that troubles are going to arise.

The other thing that the boss needs to remember is the punishment of the Lord. One day, at the end of the day, the employee and the employer will stand naked before God absolutely equal – no difference of status, for God has no favourites, no distinction, no partiality. God will say to the employer, "Answer to me for your work as an employer." God will say to the employee, "Answer to me for the work you did as an employee." Did you employ as to the Lord, and were you employed as by the Lord? The two people will stand together. What a difference there will be. They may never have sat together at a table in life; they may never even have gone into the factory by the same door, but one day they will stand in the same place. When two men remember that, they treat each other very differently.

In conclusion, may I point out there is something much deeper in these few verses 5–9 than we have looked at already: hidden in these verses is the answer to social injustice, the way that Christians can deal with social evil. For slavery was a dreadful evil. Two-thirds of the population had no rights and no income whatever, and that was a social evil. How did the early Christians tackle this social injustice? They did not start a revolution. They did not start a rebellion. They did not shout about rights. One of the subtle temptations that the church is falling for today is to think that the fight for social justice involves Christians becoming embroiled in revolution and rebellion. Christians ought to know by now that that way replaces one tyranny by another, it does not solve the situation. How then does a Christian deal with social injustice? Does he march around with banners and shout about rights? No, he undermines that injustice by injecting into it new attitudes and relationships. It may be a slower way, but it is a surer way. It was this injection of a new relationship and attitude that brought slavery crashing to the ground later. Notice that Paul is writing to a church and he says, "You slaves", "You masters". They are sitting together and that is a revolution. You did not find that in the pagan temples. If they went to the same temple, you would find the masters at one end and the slaves at the other. But Paul is saying: you are all together in this. That is as it should be. The church has no distinctions of employer and employee, no distinctions of wealthy or poor. The church is the pioneer of social justice because it brings everybody down to the same level – as sinners before God. So Paul says, "There you are, slaves and masters, together in church. Treat each other as people." That is the revolution that cracked slavery. That is the injection of a new attitude and a new relationship which undermined a social evil which collapsed. When slaves and masters were in the same fellowship and brothers in the Lord, then you had a new situation.

We have to confess before God with shame that there are not enough Christians in England to inject this kind of attitude and relationship into our trade unions, into our business circles, into our political affairs. Therefore, because we are frustrated at not having enough Christians to put the right attitude in, we are tempted to shout and march. We are tempted to try a shortcut and there isn't one.

My first prayer and target for England is to treble the

number of Christians in it. Then I think we would begin to see something happening. We just do not have enough at the moment to undermine society for the Lord. Therefore, social injustice and evil is on the march and rampant. That then is Paul's way of doing it – he took the eyes of the master and he turned the eyes of the master to the Lord; he took the eyes of the slave and turned the eyes of the slave to the Lord. Because he did that, they looked at each other with new eyes, and a new relationship was born. That is our calling and our vocation in our daily work.

THE CHRISTIAN'S WARFARE

Read Ephesians 6:10–24

A. THE ADVERSARY (11–12)
1. Satanic
2. Supernatural

B. THE ARMOUR (13–17)
1. Girdle – truth
2. Breastplate – righteousness
3. Sandals – peace
4. Shield – faith
5. Helmet – salvation
6. Sword – inspiration

C. THE ALERTNESS (18)
1. Prayer
2. Perseverance

D. THE AMBASSADOR (19–22)
1. Courage for him (19–20)
2. Comfort for them (21–22)

The benediction (23–24)

When you become a Christian you quickly make two discoveries among others, one of which is delightful and the other disturbing. The delightful discovery is that you have made a whole lot of new friends, and wherever you go you will meet Christian brothers and sisters, and after you have talked with them for five minutes you feel you have known them for such a long time. It is a wonderful circle of friends to which you now belong. The disturbing discovery is that you have made a whole lot of new enemies.

A girl once said to Charles Haddon Spurgeon, "How much of the world should I give up, now that I'm a Christian?" He replied very wisely, "Don't worry, the world will give you up." That is the problem – keeping your old friends. The Christian life is not just a walk, it is a warfare, and therefore the whole mood of the letter to the Ephesians changes at this point. You are in a conflict, a deadly struggle. The word Paul uses is "wrestle", which means hand-to-hand fighting. You are in the front line, you can't fight from a distance, you can't fire shells and hope that they land on targets some miles away. You are going to be engaged in personal conflicts and struggle in which you have to wrestle with enemies, and every Christian will know this sooner or later.

We are all at war, and if you had a comparatively peaceful life before you became a Christian, in one sense to become a Christian is to lose that peace. You are right in the front line. It is most dangerous to be a weak Christian. As in every battle, the only ones who will survive are the strong; the weak will go to the wall. A weak Christian will very quickly find that they cannot keep it up. The struggle is too great. There is only one hope of holding on and that is to be strong in the Lord. You are weak in yourself and how quickly you discover this – you struggle to be a better Christian and you fail. You never will fight and win in your own strength. So Paul writes: "Finally, my brethren, be strong in the Lord in the strength of his might." Discover how to be strong in him.

You see, God has never promised to take you out of the battle – not until you die. What he has promised is to give you the strength and the armour, all the equipment and resources that you need to win. He wants soldiers, not just servants. He wants those who will fight for him. He wants you in the front lines, so be strong in the Lord and in the strength of his might. The aim of a soldier is never to retreat.

The Roman soldiers almost regarded this principle as their religion. When Julius Caesar's troops landed on the shores of England, the first thing they did was to turn around and burn their boats (the origin of the expression "burning your boats"). So they could not retreat, they just had to come on and conquer England. It is that ambition which ought to be at the heart of every Christian soldier. I will never go back — God helping me, I will never retreat; I will never give to the enemy an inch of the ground that I have gained in Christ.

Therefore the word that is used frequently now is "stand". In relation to the enemy we are called to *stand* – to sit in relation to Christ, to walk in relationship with each other, but to stand in the face of the enemy. Now the first need is to identify the enemy. You could attack the wrong people, you could fight on the wrong front, and while you are busy fighting the wrong people the real enemy could creep around your flank finding you unaware. The real enemy is not human at all. The Christian does not regard any man or woman as his enemy. He lives at peace with all men insofar as in him lies. The real enemy is unseen, that is the problem. Now don't get me wrong, some people may make it jolly difficult for you to be a Christian: your relatives, your friends, your colleagues at work can make life very difficult indeed, but you must not wrestle with them. They are not the real enemy, and if you fight with them you are using up your energy in the wrong direction and you are liable to be caught unawares by the real foe.

The first need, then, is to realise that human beings are not our enemies. Who are the enemies? First, Paul tells us that your enemy is satanic. I can never understand a Christian who says to me: "Do you believe in a personal devil?" I just can't help believing in a personal devil – as soon as you become a Christian you seem to run up against the enemy straightaway. He just doesn't leave you alone, and the Bible teaches the existence of a devil as clearly as it teaches the existence of God – particularly at three points in the Bible: in the book of Genesis, at the beginning; in the four Gospels in the middle, and in the book of Revelation at the end. Those are the books that tell you about the devil, and that is why the devil doesn't like you to read any of them.

Alas, many caricatures of the devil have helped us to treat him as a joke. Those sort of caricature pictures of a little black demon with horns and a forked tail – the devil doesn't look like that. If he did, you would recognise him; if you saw that coming up your garden path you would slam the door. Take the devil very seriously. He is said to be like a lion, and you would not take a lion into your house lightly; you would not laugh. He is said to be like a dragon or a crocodile. A British nurse in Africa was seized by a crocodile and pulled into a river, and with great presence of mind a number of Africans there jumped in, formed a human chain and they hung on to one arm while the crocodile hung on to the other. Finally, the crocodile let go and they pulled that girl back safely, and she was alive and well – no laughing matter. The devil is like that, and Paul is going to teach that you need to pray for all the saints and pray for each other or you will get caught. He is like an old serpent. If you lived in a country where poisonous snakes are frequently found inside your house, you would not laugh, you would take it very seriously indeed. If you have had any experience with snakes, you know the sort of feelings that you ought to have about Satan.

The Bible goes on to say that he is a person of superior intelligence and strength to you. He has got the edge on you and you could never win a battle with him by yourself, and you are up against this evil being. Don't you find, when you really try to follow Christ, that you get the sense that someone tries to stop you? Someone who knows you inside out, someone who knows how to get hold of you – and with everything you try, somehow there seems a barrier, a blockage; you want to serve God and yet there seems to be an enemy. There is an enemy and he is described in the Bible as a ruler, the prince, the god of this world. That is why you didn't have any bother with him before you became a Christian. You were born in his domain. He had a complete grip on you – you did what he told you to, and you enjoyed it, and he just rubbed his hands. When you became a Christian he hated you. You are a traitor to Satan and he will deal with you as a traitor. When Christ saved you, he saved you from the power of the devil. He translated you from the kingdom of darkness into his own kingdom. He got you free, he had to break some chains, he had to open a prison door – and the chains had been put there by Satan – and your chains fell off and you rose, went forth, and followed Jesus. Satan will do everything he can to stop you. Satan is no match for God. He knows that, therefore he doesn't try to stop God, but he is a match for God's people, and all his attack will be directed not against God but against God's people. For that is how he can try to delay the kingdom coming.

Secondly, not only are we up against a satanic enemy, we are up against supernatural hosts – armies. It is not just one devil but many demons. Now of course, people have been laughing for a long time at the idea that evil spirits exist. Some used to say, many years ago, that when the Bible talked about evil spirits possessing a person, that was because they had no psychiatric training in those days – that it was their word for schizophrenia, manic depression or some other mental illness. But don't you believe a word of it. There are such mental illnesses, but they have nothing to do with what we are looking at now. Perfectly healthy Christians, balanced and integrated people, physically, mentally, emotionally, spiritually, find themselves having to cope with evil spirits.

More recently, opinion has changed remarkably about this, because we have begun to see a flooding back of interest in evil spirits. Spiritism is on the increase, interest in the occult is increasingly seen in our newspapers, magazines and on the television. People are dabbling in magic. Almost every week I come across someone who has been playing with evil spirits. They are only too real, and people are coming under the grip of such evil powers, demonic forces.

Paul writes about supernatural beings, evil spirits, as being in charge of the world: politics, commerce, science, art, education. According to the Bible, these are in the grip of principalities and powers. Do you find that an astonishing assertion?

Think back to the long conflict in Northern Ireland. That was the strongest part of the United Kingdom spiritually. Northern Ireland was a place where people still went to church. Northern Ireland sent more money and men to the mission field than any other part of the UK in proportion to its population, and the devil hated Northern Ireland – that was what was happening. The devil got men so in his grip that they would not even listen to reason, they were blindly going on bringing the whole of Northern Ireland into disrepute so that the very name of Christ was suffering. Can you see that? I can take one situation after another in the world and you will find, again and again, that the devil is trying to close the door to the Christian gospel. Wherever Christ is strong, he is strong too, and seeking to do something. All the hosts of wickedness in heavenly places come into the picture. I believe that explains why flesh and blood can't solve situations. It is neutralising the gospel of our Lord Jesus Christ. That is just one illustration of how supernatural forces have this world in control. Why is it that we just can't get peace? Why is it that people can't live together? This is what Paul is talking about.

Therefore, these enemies are not only supernatural and satanic, they are spiritual. You can't fight them with any weapons but spiritual ones. You can't fight them with military weapons; you could send the entire British army but they can't touch the devil. Why is it that we have wars to end wars, yet never seem to end war? I read that Adolf Hitler in 1937 began to dabble in spiritism and evil spirits. Do you wonder that Europe was plunged into the holocaust of suffering that it was? But now in peacetime we are dabbling in the same things and we expect to get away with it. You can't fight them physically, you can't fight them mentally, because it is not a war of ideas. This explains why it is so difficult to fight, because you can't get hold of them. Where are they? Where are these evil spirits? Paul says they are in heaven, and that is the problem.

There are spiritual hosts of wickedness not down below in hell but above in heavenly places, and as soon as you were made to sit in the heavenly places, you came in contact with them because that is where they are. The real conflict is going on in the heavenly places—that is where it has got to be fought and that is where the battle is happening. Conflicts on earth are just the overspill of what is happening there; that is why you can't see these enemies, you can't hear them, they are unseen, they are spiritual, in the heavenly places.

The battle in Britain is going on apace—indeed I hardly need to persuade you of this battle. We can't sort it out by appealing to human beings to act, because it is not flesh and blood behind it. It will need spiritual weapons. You know, the devil hates me for teaching this and I am conscious of that – he just hates it. He wants you to go on fighting on a physical level, at a mental level, but Paul says put on the whole armour of God.

Paul is writing this while chained to a Roman soldier, and as he writes this letter he looks up and he looks at that solider and that soldier is there as a Roman not to give an inch; he is there to defend. Therefore he has dressed very carefully that morning. He has put everything on that he needs to put on so that he won't give an inch. Paul, looking at the soldier, writes to these Christians at Ephesus and tells them how they need to be equipped. You need to put on the armour of God. You haven't got any of your own; you couldn't defend yourself against Satan, but put on the armour of God. Do you remember reading in *The Pilgrims Progress* that when Pilgrim is fitted out with the armour and he says, "What's all this for?", they say, "You are going to face an enemy, Apollyon, you must put this on – you need it." The pilgrim has never worn armour before and puts it all on, piece by piece, and very shortly afterwards he is in a valley and he is fighting for his life.

Notice that we have got to put it all on. It is utterly silly to put on a helmet and leave your chest exposed, or to take a shield but nothing else. You will need every little bit of God's armour because the enemy goes for the point where there is no protection. The phrase "tempted in all points" is a very interesting one. It does not mean that Jesus knew every temptation we know. The word "point" means the point at which you can get through – a weak point in the armour; a chink. Jesus was tempted in all points and so will we be. If you have left something off, that is where the devil will come. Put on then the whole armour of God – complete coverage.

Let us see what it is. The first thing you will need is a belt. Most soldiers have a belt. On it they usually hang their guns, their ammunition. In those days they used to hang their sword. You will need a belt, and a Roman soldier wore a wide leather belt studded with metal, and from it hung the scabbard for his sword. The belt held him together – gripped him, held his tunic in so that it didn't flap about, but it gave him freedom of movement so he was in the grip of this belt. I heard of an Irish farm labourer who, whenever he was going to lift a heavy load, would take his belt up one hole, bracing himself for the effort, holding himself together – pulled his belt in, and then he got under the sack to lift it. A soldier does that. The first thing a soldier does, going on duty, is to brace himself with a belt. Paul is saying that the first thing you need is to be gripped by truth, held by truth, absolutely in the grip of reality. That is the very first thing you will need. Belt on the truth – that is the first piece of equipment. Then, whatever happens, you will say: "I'm in the grip of the truth. Whatever you say to me, I am held by the truth that braces me for the battle."

The second piece of equipment you will need is something to cover your heart. Soldiers' hearts can fail them in the middle of battle; their morale can go. Paul is teaching us that if you want to keep your morale high, keep your morals high. For the one thing that the enemy can do to your heart is to tell you that you are not worthy to fight, and the heart will go out of you. The breastplate covers the heart. What do you need to protect your heart? Righteousness, uprightness – the devil loves to be able to point and say, "You are not what you should be" – and the heart will go out of you in the fight. The breastplate of righteousness to protect your heart – otherwise if your morals go down then your morale goes down; your heart fails you and the breastplate is of no use.

The third item of equipment is for your feet: sandals. Now there has been a lot of debate about the meaning of this. Sandals we think of as something to walk with or even run with, but the Roman soldier had special sandals. They had spikes in the soles and they were sandals to stay put. In other words, when you were going to wrestle, you dug both feet in and in hand-to-hand combat fighting they couldn't move you. Your feet were literally anchored to the ground – sandals were spiked to hold there. You hold yourself by standing on the gospel of peace. That is amazing, to use peace to fight a war, but Paul means remember above all not to stoop to your enemy's attack. He is going to war with you, but you remember that your aim is peace. I can think of so many stories of men who have been attacked by Satan but remembered that they were shod with the gospel of peace. I think of a Japanese Christian when he was thrown out of college as a student because he was a Christian and the professors had him before them and said, "We do not want you in our college, you must go." He remembered that he had his feet shod with the preparation of the gospel of peace. He went up to his professors and he kissed them in love. He didn't fight them, he didn't resent it, he didn't give back what he had been given, he just kissed them goodbye in love.

Paul, as a prisoner in Rome chained to a Roman soldier, didn't say, "What have you done to me? Why are you keeping me here?" He wasn't resentful. He remembered that on his feet he had the gospel of peace and so he would talk to the Roman soldier, pray for him, and he won those soldiers for Christ. That is the best form of defence – to attack with the gospel of peace. Just stay put. I am not going to fight the same with satanic weapons, I'm not going to come down to his level of fighting, I am not going to hit below the belt, even if he does. My feet are on the gospel of peace.

The fourth thing you will need is a shield. We sometimes see news broadcasts showing things set alight and flung at someone. No wonder the police and soldiers have used shields. If you are having a bomb thrown at you, then you would want something to hold. In the biblical days, the equivalent was a fiery dart. It was a short spear or arrow soaked in pitch and set alight, and that could really do some damage. It was just like throwing a "molotov cocktail", and the devil doesn't mind throwing equivalent things at you.

There is only one thing that will deal with it. In those days the Roman soldier had a big, soft wooden shield. He had little, round metal ones when he was on the attack but when he was on the defence he had an oblong wooden shield big enough for his whole body to crouch behind. The soft wood caught the darts, absorbed the fire and put it out. Paul is thinking of that shield because that is the word he uses here. Above all, get behind the "shield of faith". Whatever the devil throws at you, say, "I believe; I trust." Whatever fiery darts he throws, say, "I believe – my faith is not affected," and your faith absorbs the attack of the devil.

Next you will need something to protect your head. Now, your head is that with which you think. This is your beliefs, your doctrine, your understanding of God. The protection of your head will be salvation. You can get lost in theology, lost in philosophy, and the devil can twist your thinking round and round until you don't know what you believe. The one thing that will keep your head protected is to gear all your thinking to salvation, to your Saviour – to the things that make for salvation. Let that be the centre of your thinking and the devil can't attack your head.

Finally, there is the only item of equipment that Paul mentions which is not an item of defence. The belt, breastplate, shield, sandals and helmet are all to defend yourself, but there is one item with which to attack. It is a little Roman sword, quite short and broad, with a cutting edge down both sides and a ridge down the middle. So often in the Bible this term is used of words. The word of God is sharper than a two-edged sword. You find the picture of Jesus in the book of Revelation with a tongue like this – a tongue that cuts.

The sword of the Spirit is a Christian's tongue. It may be pulled from the belt of truth as it were, but we get it mixed up when we think of the sword of the Spirit as the Bible. It does not mean throw the book at him. It means: let the Spirit guide your tongue. He may bring you a text from the Bible. He may bring you some other words. The sword of the Spirit is what the Spirit gives you to say in that moment under attack. It is a very sharp sword to him. That is what Jesus used. When the devil attacked Jesus in the wilderness, Jesus said, "Have you not read, you shall not tempt the Lord your God" – and he used his tongue and the devil did not like that sword. The sword of the Spirit is the tongue and you will need it, and the Spirit will give you what to say.

Do you realise that in all this Paul is saying: put on Jesus. Jesus is the truth. Jesus is our righteousness. Jesus is the author and the perfecter of our faith. Jesus is our salvation. Put on Jesus, and you are more than a match for Satan. Now we come to v. 18 which I call the alertness. A weak soldier is of no use. A soldier without his armour is no use, and likewise a soldier who falls asleep is of no use. That is one of the most serious crimes in the army – to be put on sentry duty and to fall asleep. You can be court-martialled for that – to be drowsy when you should be alert. Edinburgh Castle looks impregnable, but twice in its history it has been taken and each time it was because a sentry was not watching – and the devil will take you if you are not watching.

How do you watch? Funnily enough, the Christian watches by closing his eyes – that is how you watch for the devil. There is no point in watching for him with your eyes, you can't see him. He is a supernatural, spiritual being; you will never see the devil with your eyes, not in this life anyway. When you close your eyes you begin to see, especially when you close them in prayer. This is the way to keep alert. The greatest weapon you have against Satan is prayer. You pray: "Deliver us from evil." Really, Jesus said "Deliver us from the evil one." I wish we could change the Lord's Prayer back to what Jesus said: "Lead us not into temptation but deliver us from the evil one." Satan trembles when he sees the weakest saint upon his knees. There is no weapon you have which causes him more anxiety.

Therefore one could say that the one thing Satan will try to do is to get you to stop praying. It is the one thing he will put as his top priority in your life, and if he can do that he knows you will be weak. This is to be a total strategy: pray at all times. There is a slight difference between the phrase "all the time" and "at all times". You can't be praying consciously all the time. You would be neglecting other duties. You can't pray while you sleep and there are certain other situations requiring your whole concentration. "Pray at all times" means whenever you have a need, whenever you face a situation.

I know Christian surgeons who, before they go into the operating theatre, having put on the mask, the gloves and the robe, go into a little corner and they pray. Then they go into the operating theatre and they need all their concentration, all their thoughts on the patient – but they have prayed at all times. They have prayed about their work. It means at any time, at any place, pray, because the devil doesn't just come to you Sunday mornings. In fact, he rarely comes on Sunday mornings or Sunday evenings. Monday morning is his favourite morning. He seems sometimes to take a weekend off and then start work when we do. He will come to you at the most unexpected time. Pray at that time, at all times, right at the moment you need. Christ has opened a door into the throne room of the universe that Satan cannot shut.

Prayer is the quickest way to deal with it. We are to pray in the Spirit. The opposite of that is praying in the flesh. Here are just two little thoughts: praying in the flesh is usually praying after you have got into the trouble; praying in the Spirit is praying before. To pray in the Spirit is to prepare. Most people pray in the flesh after they have got into a jam. Another difference is that praying in the Spirit is praying the words he gives you; praying in the flesh can be praying in your own words, and there are many other differences.

Pray in the Spirit at all times, with all prayer. Do you notice this little word "all"? All times, all prayer, all the saints. Do you realise that your prayer could keep somebody out of Satan's hands today? That is why we don't say, "Lead *me* not into temptation and deliver *me* from the evil one," but, "Lead *us*..." – all the saints. If we pray for other Christians, we are helping them to win the battle, and it has got to be with all perseverance. Battles are not won in a moment. Sometimes it will be a hard grind, and you have got to go on and on. The Christian life is not always glamorous or spectacular. Sometimes it is just a long, hard grind and a pull with all perseverance, making supplication for the saints.

In vv. 19–22, we come to the ambassador. Paul is humble enough to say he needs their prayers: "I am an ambassador for Christ but I am in chains, will you pray for me?" Now what are his two concerns? These should be our concerns in prayer. First of all he asks for prayer for courage. Not for safety, not for comfort, not for health, not even for release, but that he may have the courage to speak for the Lord where he is. That is the first prayer to pray for a Christian soldier, not that he may be comfortable or safe but that he may have courage.

I remember reading a book by Daniel Poling—have you heard of him? His son went off to the war – from the United States, as a chaplain to the forces. Every night, Daniel and his wife would get down on their knees and say, "Lord, keep our boy safe. Bring him back to us safe and sound." Now that is praying in the flesh, because that is a desire of the flesh. It is an instinctive desire to have your child back. Then, one day, Daniel Poling and his wife realised that this was a prayer in the flesh, that it was the kind of prayer that anybody would pray, whether they were a believer or not. They were praying that all the bullets that were flying would hit someone else, and they realised that was the wrong prayer. So they changed their prayers and they began to pray, "Lord, give our boy courage. Give him the courage to witness for you whatever happens, in whatever circumstance. We want him to be a witness for you, whether he comes back to us or not." Do you know what happened to their son? During the war, a troop ship was torpedoed and went down in the middle of the Atlantic and there were not enough lifebelts to go around. There were four chaplains on board, who had life jackets, but they took their life jackets off, gave them to other men, linked arms, and went down on the ship singing, "Nearer My God to Thee". It has been put on an American stamp. You can buy a stamp today with those four men on board going down on the ship. Their prayer was answered: "Pray that utterance may be given me in opening my mouth boldly." Soldiers shouldn't pray for safety, or comfort or ease, they should pray for courage. Just as a weak soldier is of no use, a cowardly soldier is of no use either. Pray for boldness – look at the word "boldly" – even in chains, to be brave.

I think too of Martin Niemoller in a little cell in a concentration camp. What could he do? He prayed for the courage to open his mouth boldly but he was in solitary confinement; there was no-one there to talk to and the guard only came in once or twice a day. Then he noticed, high in one wall of the cell, a little opening, a sort of ventilation grate. He discovered it opened on to the yard where the other prisoners took their exercise, so whenever he heard them exercising in the yard, he would climb on his little bed and put his mouth to the grille and recite texts from the Bible, one after the other. As each prisoner walked past, a word of God came out of the grating. Courage, boldness – and he still got that courage. Years later, his wife died in a car crash, which he survived. He still had the same courage – a bold soldier, a brave man. He had been through one experience after another with courage.

That is what our prayer should be—not that we may all be happy, comfortable, wealthy, and healthy, but that we may be bold – brave soldiers fighting well. Paul is saying: pray for courage for me and I am going to send someone to encourage you. "Encourage" means to put courage into someone, to make them bold. His imprisonment might have discouraged them, and they might have felt it could be them next, but he was sending someone to tell them that he was well, that he was able to win people for Christ there. He was sending Tychichus, that beloved brother, to put courage into them too. How petty our prayers can be, how selfish, how much in the flesh. Pray in the Spirit that I may be given boldness, that you may be encouraged, that we may be brave soldiers.

Paul finishes the letter as he began it. He began it by saying "grace and peace" and finishes by saying "peace and grace". These are the two great themes of Jew and Gentile. They both wished for it and longed for it. The Jew kept saying "Peace" to a fellow Jew, and the Gentile said "Grace" to his fellow Gentile, and Paul is teaching that you can have both in Christ – peace and grace. He finishes with a lovely phrase, "With all who love the Lord Jesus, with a love undying." A soldier is called upon to fight for love of country, but a Christian soldier is called to fight for love of Jesus. "Love undying" – Jesus loved his own and he loved them till the end, with love undying. You might die in the service of Christ, but your love should never die. Love undying is prepared to die in other ways – to die to self, to die even to life, but the love will never die.

Sir Monier Monier-Williams, Professor of Sanskrit at Oxford, lay dying in Cannes in the south of France in April 1899. As he lay there, he was asked this, "Is there anything you want?"

He replied, "Jesus loves me and I love Jesus, what more do I want?"

For more of David Pawson's teaching,
including DVDs and CDs, go to
www.davidpawson.com

FOR FREE DOWNLOADS
www.davidpawson.org

Lightning Source UK Ltd.
Milton Keynes UK
UKHW021854040620
364445UK00012B/2115